BRITISH DIESEL AND ELECTRIC LOCOMOTIVES ABROAD

A SECOND LIFE OVERSEAS

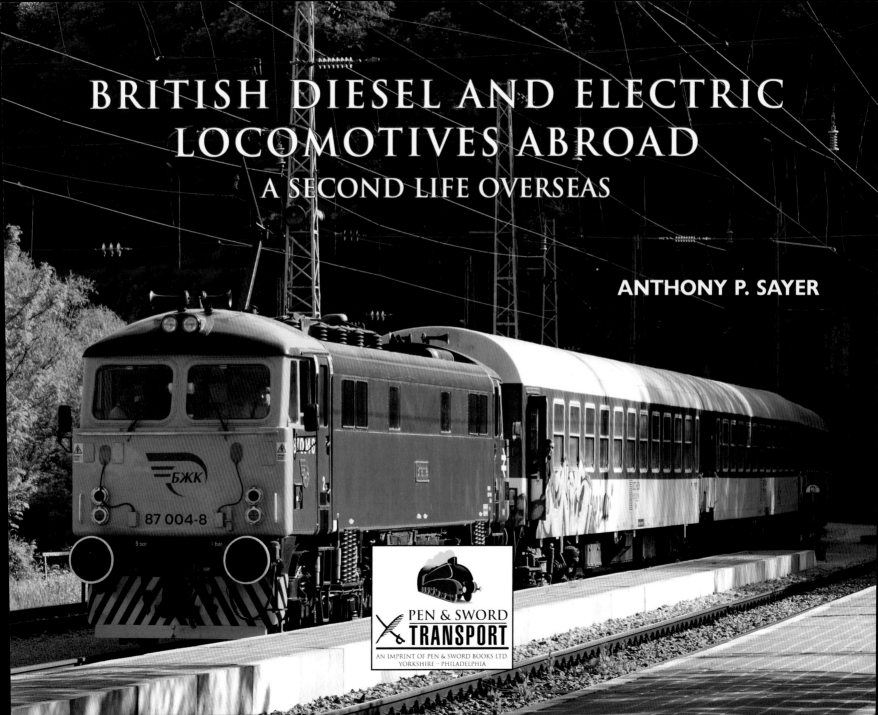

BRITISH DIESEL AND ELECTRIC
LOCOMOTIVES ABROAD
A SECOND LIFE OVERSEAS

ANTHONY P. SAYER

PEN & SWORD
TRANSPORT

AN IMPRINT OF PEN & SWORD BOOKS LTD.
YORKSHIRE – PHILADELPHIA

First published in Great Britain in 2020 by
Pen and Sword Transport
An imprint of
Pen & Sword Books Ltd
Yorkshire - Philadelphia

ISBN 978 1 52674 469 2

Typeset by Aura Technology and Software Services, India
Printed and bound in China through Printworks Global Ltd.

Pen & Sword Books Ltd incorporates the Imprints of Pen & Sword Books Archaeology,
Atlas, Aviation, Battleground, Discovery, Family History, History, Maritime, Military,
Naval, Politics, Railways, Select, Transport, True Crime, Fiction, Frontline Books, Leo
Cooper, Praetorian Press, Seaforth Publishing, Wharncliffe and White Owl.

For a complete list of Pen & Sword titles please contact

PEN & SWORD BOOKS LIMITED
47 Church Street, Barnsley, South Yorkshire, S70 2AS, England
E-mail: enquiries@pen-and-sword.co.uk
Website: www.pen-and-sword.co.uk

or

PEN AND SWORD BOOKS
1950 Lawrence Rd, Havertown, PA 19083, USA
E-mail: Uspen-and-sword@casematepublishers.com
Website: www.penandswordbooks.com

Cover photo (upper): 37071, 37162, 37010, 37376, Eurre, France, 12 June 2000.

Cover photo (lower): 87033, Pirdop, Bulgaria, 4 May 2010.

Title Page photo: 87004 at Veliko Tarnovo, Bulgaria, on 3 May 2010 with the PTG 'Magnificent Seven to the Black Sea' railtour.

Back cover photo: 87009, plus 86701/231/234/213/702/235 at Razdelna on 3 May 2016 ready for movement to Ruse. A British locomotive about to haul a newly imported contingent of British locomotives across Bulgaria!

Contents

Preface

This album was originally intended to be a purely photographic overview of British-built main-line diesel and electric locomotives which managed to find further useful employment overseas following the completion of their careers in the United Kingdom. However, such was the volume of information collected regarding the exported locomotives and their deployment over the past twenty years that I thought it would be interesting to mix-and-match the factual and the pictorial into a more detailed history of the locomotives that have worked in Europe as far afield as France, the Netherlands, Spain, Italy, Kosovo, Hungary, Romania, Bulgaria and Croatia since 1998.

My early photographs were black and white, followed from 2003 by digital images. Slides were taken pre-2003 but such was the quality of these images that they did not satisfactorily scan across to digital and, therefore, have not been used here.

Dates in the text and photograph captions are provided in the 25 March 2015 format; however, for tabular information the 25/03/15 format is used to conserve space.

January 2020

Acknowledgements

Much of the information contained within this book has been assembled through personal observations and information derived from many contacts 'on the ground' over the years (many of whom wish to remain anonymous for understandable reasons). Particular thanks must go to Keith Butler, Keith Harper and Fraser Wilson for their help with regards to the Class 37s and 58s in France and Spain.

Internet photographic sites have provided additional supporting information concerning the latest locations and liveries of particular locomotives.

Photographs are my own except where specified. My thanks go to Jose-Ramon Corbacho, Keith Harper, Keith Butler and Miroslav Georgiev for their very interesting contributions and help with filling some of my photographic gaps.

Abbreviations

A   Austria.
ACTS   Afzet Container Transport Systeem (Holland).
ADIF   Administrador de Infraestructuras Ferroviaria (Spain).
AVE   Alta Velocidad Española (Spain).
B   Belgium.
BG   Bulgaria.
BR   British Rail.
BZK   ВБЛГАРСКА ЖЕЛЕЗОПЪТНА КОМПАНИЯ (Bulgarian Railway Company) (Bulgaria).
CEAAV   Consorzio Europeo Armamento Alta Velocita (Italy).
CFD   Compagnie Chemin de Fer Departementaux (subsequently CFD Industrie) (France).
CRS   Continental Railway Solution (Hungary).
D   Germany.
DB   Deutsche Bahn (German Railways).
DRS   Direct Rail Services (UK).
E   Spain.
ETF   Eurovia Travaux Ferroviaires (France).
EVN   European Vehicle Number.
EWS   English, Welsh and Scottish Railway (UK) (also EW&S).

F   France.
GIF   Gestor de Infraestructuras Ferroviarias (Spain).
HR   Croatia (Hrvatska).
HŽ   Hrvatske Željeznice (Croatian Railways).
HSL   High-Speed Line.
HU   Hungary.
I   Italy.
LAV   Línea de Alta Velocidad (Spain).
LGV   Ligne à Grande Vitesse (France).
NL   Netherlands/Holland.
RENFE   Red Nacional de los Ferrocarriles Españoles (Spanish National Railways).
RO   Romania.
SNCF   Société Nationale des Chemins de Fer Français (French National Railways).
TaR   Transagent Rail (Croatia).
TaŠ   Transagent Špedicija (Croatia).
TSO   Travaux du Sud Ouest (France).
UIC   Union Internationale des Chemin de Fer (International Union of Railways).

Introduction

This book quite specifically covers main-line diesel and electric locomotives built in the UK which have subsequently moved across to mainland Europe for further use or to support other locomotives in revenue-earning service (e.g. spare parts donors). There are, of course, exceptions to every rule and 56007 and 56018 have been included despite being constructed in Romania (as sub-contracted by Brush).

Deliberately not included are locomotives sent abroad purely for exhibition purposes, locomotives 'exported' for equipment testing, and locomotives associated with the 'near Continent' Channel Tunnel activities, for example for initial construction work (Class 20s) and subsequent everyday operations (Class 92s).

The year 1999 has been used as the effective start point, partly for my convenience (i.e. photograph availability!) but also on the basis that this was the year that really saw the commencement of volume-usage of British locomotives abroad. For completeness, however, it is worth quickly referencing the main-line diesel locomotives which operated in Europe prior to 1999.

The earliest transfer of a British main-line locomotive abroad was 6000 (subsequently E26000 *Tommy*); this locomotive was loaned to the Dutch railways over the period 1947-52. Other early transfers represented the isolated sales of redundant assets, for example: seven Class 77 electric locomotives (E27000-6) to the Netherlands in 1969 (for the princely sum of £37,750 including spares); HS4000 *Kestrel* to Russia in 1971; and five Class 14 diesel-hydraulics to Belgium in 1975 (D9505/34) and Spain in 1982 (D9515/48/9).

1. France: CFD Class 20s

BR sold four Class 20 locomotives to CFD (Compagnie Chemin de Fer Departementaux, subsequently CFD Industrie) who moved them to France (via Poole and Cherbourg) in June/July 1992, following overhaul, modifications and repainting at BREL Crewe Works. On arrival in France, all locomotives had their tyres re-profiled to meet local requirements and also received new light clusters. These locomotives were based at Autun and operated freight trains on the Cravant Bazarnes-Avallon-Saulieu-Autun-Étang-Montchanin route in Central France.

The locomotives were numbered 2001-2004 and painted in a distinctive orange livery. SNCF type-approval details were applied to the locomotive bodysides.

The Class 20s returned to the UK during August/September 2005 via Southampton after a number of years of declining use following the purchase of CFD by SNCF subsidiary VFLI.

Summary:-

Loco No.	Prepared at	CFD No.	SNCF Approval No.	Ex-UK	Returned UK	Liveries
20035	Crewe Works	2001	AT3 DJ 053	09/07/92	28/08/05	CFD Orange
Noted: Cherbourg Yard, 22/07/92.						
20063	Crewe Works	2002	AT3 DJ 054	09/07/92	28/08/05	CFD Orange
Noted: Cherbourg Yard, 22/07/92.						
20139	Crewe Works	2003	AT3 DJ 051	03/06/92	10/09/05	CFD Orange
Initially sent to Trappes, Paris for wheel-turning, then Vitry for static testing, followed by road testing between Montchanin and Cercy-la-Tour 07-08/07/92.						
20228	Crewe Works	2004	AT3 DJ 052	09/07/92	03/09/05	CFD Orange
Noted: Cherbourg Yard, 22/07/92.						

20063 (2002) and 20035 (2001), Avallon, 13 August 1996. Double-headed Class 20s working a freight service from Saulieu to Cravant Bazarnes consisting predominantly of timber logs; the train spent an hour shunting the yard at Avallon before proceeding to Cravant Bazarnes. Note that the original reporting discs have been removed, replaced by new light clusters.

20139 (2003), Autun, 13 August 1996. Stabled outside the part-roundhouse at Autun. 20139 and 20228 had their headcode boxes completely removed during their preparatory overhaul at Crewe Works, these being superceded by new light clusters.

20139 (2003) and 20228 (2004), Auxerre St.Gervais, 8 August 1998. 'Along Different Lines' (ADL) 'The CFD Chopper Tour'.

20063 (2002) and 20035 (2001), Autun, 16 October 1999. ADL 'Choppers and Tractors' tour.

2. Kosovo: Class 20s

DRS (Direct Rail Services) Class 20 locomotives 20901-3 were sent from the UK to Kosovo in September 1999 as part of the 'Kosovo Train for Life' initiative, with the Class 20s actually hauling the train in parts of the transit through Europe. The 'Train for Life' initiative provided humanitarian aid for the local people following the Kosovo War.

The Class 20s were hauled through the Channel Tunnel to Calais Fréthun on 17 September 1999 and attached to their train a day later. The route through Europe spanning 18-27 September 1999 was: Calais-Lille-Aachen (to pick up more aid wagons)-Berlin-Dresden-Decin-Prague-Kuty-Sturovo-Budapest-Bekescsaba-Craiova-Giurgiu-Ruse-Sofia-Dupnica-Strimon-Thessaloniki-Skopje-Kosovo Polje.

Once in Kosovo, the Class 20s were deployed shunting further aid trains in support of the UN/KFOR (United Nations/Kosovo Protection Force) humanitarian effort, together with moving essential reconstruction materials, up to January 2000. They were subsequently stored at Skopje prior to returning to the UK via Thessoloniki port to Marchwood Military Port near Southampton.

Summary:-

Loco No.	Prepared at	Ex-UK	Returned UK	Liveries
20901	Carlisle Kingmoor	17/09/99	08/04/00	DRS DRSlogo
20902	Carlisle Kingmoor	17/09/99	08/04/00	DRS DRSlogo
20903	Carlisle Kingmoor	17/09/99	08/04/00	DRS DRSlogo

3. France: LGV Méditerranée Class 37s

It was the acceleration of high-speed line (HSL) construction in mainland Europe which really sparked the movement of British locomotives abroad in any volume, earning useful revenue from otherwise redundant assets. During the period June to September 1999, EWS (English Welsh & Scottish Railway) moved forty Class 37 locomotives to France, via the Channel Tunnel, to assist with the construction of the LGV (Ligne à Grande Vitesse) Méditerranée from St.Marcel-lès-Valence (near Valence) to Marseilles. They were all based at Eurre (adjacent to the Livron-sur-Drôme - Crest line) and operated northwards on the construction 'trace' to the St.Marcel-lès-Valence TGV station, and, southwards to the Lapalud loops with the objective of meeting up with the construction teams working northwards from the Cheval-Blanc LGV Base (near Cavaillon) during April 2000. However, the northbound Cheval-Blanc team ran late and as a result the contract for the EWS Class 37s operating from Eurre was extended from 28 April to 1 September 2000; as a consequence the Eurre team continued with construction work for another twelve miles south of Lapalud beyond Mondragon.

To assist with the extended contract, two locomotives with major defects (37073 and 37298) were replaced by 37888 and 37896, these two being forwarded through the Channel Tunnel on 11 May 2000, together with an additional supply of spares. Following failures with other Class 37s, the EWS-liveried 37298 was repaired and returned to traffic.

All of the forty-two Class 37s retained their motley selection of British liveries whilst in France.

All locomotives were returned to the UK between July and October 2000, many never to work again. The first returnees, 37513 and 37686, arrived back at Dollands Moor on 16 July 2000. Eight more followed during July 2000 with ten in August, and another eight in September. The remaining fourteen returned in October, the final pair being 37510/5 which returned home on 22 October 2000. 37800/88 saw further service in Spain – see Section 4.

Summary:-

Loco No.	Liveries/logos	Prepared at	Ex-UK	Arr Eurre Base	Returned UK
37010	dpml(r) nlogo	ML	03/09/99	06/09/99	11/10/00
37037	dgrfl nlogo	TO	27/08/99	30/08/99	14/08/00
37046	dpml(r) nlogo	OC	20/09/99	24/09/99	11/08/00
37058	dpml(r) nlogo	EH	02/08/99	06/08/99	19/08/00

Loco No.	Liveries/logos	Prepared at	Ex-UK	Arr Eurre Base	Returned UK
37069	**dpml(r) nlogo**	**BS**	**15/07/99**	**30/07/99**	**10/10/00**
37071	**dpml(r) nlogo**	**TO**	**13/07/99**	**26/07/99**	**10/10/00**
Noted en route: Avignon, 13/07/99.					
37073	**dgrfl trlogo**	**TO**	**13/07/99**	**26/07/99**	**18/10/00**
Noted en route: Avignon, 13/07/99.					
Collision damage to No.2 end sustained at Eurre Base. Earliest date noted stored at Eurre Base: 14/03/00. Not used again in France.					
37074	**mll mllogo**	**TO**	**16/09/99**	**24/09/99**	**04/08/00**
37077	**mll mllogo**	**OC**	**20/09/99**	**24/09/99**	**19/07/00**
Visited Avignon depot in 02/00 for a cylinder liner replacement. Departed Eurre: 11/07/00.					
37100	**dgrfl trlogo**	**TO**	**20/08/99**	**24/08/99**	**19/07/00**
Departed Eurre: 11/07/00.					
37133	**dpml(r) nlogo**	**EH**	**28/06/99**	**01/07/99**	**14/09/00**
Noted en route: Avignon, 29/06/99.					
37146	**dpml(r) nlogo**	**CF**	**23/08/99**	**26/08/99**	**08/09/00**
37162	**dpml nlogo**	**TO**	**23/07/99**	**30/07/99**	**13/09/00**
37170	**dpml(r) trlogo**	**TO**	**02/08/99**	**06/08/99**	**06/10/00**
37196	**dpml(r) nlogo**	**TO**	**09/07/99**	**15/07/99**	**08/09/00**
Noted en route: Avignon, 09/07/99.					
37221	**dgrfl trlogo**	**TO**	**27/08/99**	**30/08/99**	**09/08/00**
37238	**dgrfl nlogo**	**XX**	**02/07/99**	**16/07/99**	**14/08/00**
Noted en route: Avignon, 06/07/99.					
37250	**dgrfl trlogo**	**TO**	**16/07/99**	**19/07/99**	**14/09/00**
37261	**dgrfl spdlogo**	**TO**	**18/08/99**	**23/08/99**	**21/07/00**
37293	**mll mllogo**	**CD**	**13/07/99**	**27/07/99**	**04/08/00**
Noted en route: Avignon, 14/07/99.					

Loco No.	Liveries/logos	Prepared at	Ex-UK	Arr Eurre Base	Returned UK
37294	dpml(r) nlogo	ML	25/08/99	27/08/99	09/08/00
37298	ewsl(r) ewslogo(rhc)	XX	26/08/99	30/08/99	11/10/00

Auxiliary generator flashover. Earliest/latest dates noted stored at Eurre Base: 01/02/00 and 04/05/00. Subsequently repaired and noted working again by 13/06/00.

Used as backdrop to Eurre 'farewell' ceremony 06/09/00.

37376	dgrfl nlogo	TE	18/08/99	23/08/99	06/10/00
37510	icl iclogo	OC	23/08/99	26/08/99	22/10/00

Wheelset issues. Earliest/latest dates noted stored at Eurre Base: 18/03/00 and 14/06/00. Unlikely this loco ever worked again in France.

37513	lhl lhlogo	CF	16/09/99	23/09/99	16/07/00

Wheelset issues.

Departed Eurre: 10/07/00.

37515	dgrfl metlogo	XX	28/06/99	01/07/99	22/10/00

Noted en route: Avignon, 29/06/99.

Wheelset issues. Earliest/latest dates noted stored at Eurre Base: 12/06/00 and 14/06/00. Unlikely this loco worked again in France.

37671	dgrfl trlogo	CF	25/08/99	27/08/99	04/10/00
37672	dgrfl trlogo	XX	28/06/99	01/0/799	20/10/00

Noted en route: Avignon, 29/06/99.

37683	dgrfl trlogo	XX	16/07/99	19/07/99	20/10/00
37685	icl iclogo	TE	01/09/99	09/09/99	11/08/00

Bogie change at Eurre 05/01/00.

37686	dgrfl conlogo	BS	09/07/99	15/07/99	16/07/00

Noted en route: Avignon: 09/07/99.

Defective alternator. Earliest/latest dates noted stored at Eurre Base: 12/04/00 and 14/06/00. Unlikely this loco worked again in France.

Departed Eurre: 10/07/00.

37693	dgrfl trlogo	DR	02/07/99	16/07/99	19/08/00

Noted en route at Avignon, 06/07/99.

37696	dgrfl trlogo	OC	27/07/99	30/07/99	19/07/00

Departed Eurre: 12/07/00.

Loco No.	Liveries/logos	Prepared at	Ex-UK	Arr Eurre Base	Returned UK
37708	**dgrfl petlogo**	**CF**	**20/08/99**	**24/08/99**	**20/07/00**
Departed Eurre: 13/07/00.					
37796	**dgrfl collogo**	**XX**	**26/08/99**	**30/08/99**	**21/07/00**
37800	**dgrfl mllogo**	**BS**	**03/08/99**	**05/08/99**	**20/07/00**
Departed Eurre: 13/07/00.					
37803	**mll mllogo**	**XX**	**01/09/99**	**09/09/99**	**08/09/00**
37888	**dgrfl nlogo**	**EH**	**11/05/00**	**?**	**20/10/00**
37890	**dgrfl mllogo**	**CF**	**13/07/99**	**27/07/99**	**10/09/00**
Noted en route: Avignon, 14/07/99.					
37891	**dgrfl mllogo**	**BS**	**03/08/99**	**05/08/99**	**04/10/00**
37894	**dgrfl collogo**	**TE**	**03/09/99**	**06/09/99**	**19/07/00**
Departed Eurre: 12/07/00.					
37896	**dgrfl trlogo**	**EH**	**11/05/00**	**?**	**13/09/00**

Abbreviations:

Livery details: dgrfl: Double-Grey Railfreight, dpml: Departmental Grey, dpml(r): Revised Departmental Grey/Yellow ('Dutch'), icl: Inter-City, lhl: Loadhaul, mll: Mainline.

Logo details: collogo: Coal, iclogo: Inter-City, metlogo: Metals, mllogo: Mainline, petlogo: Petroleum, spdlogo: Speedlink, trlogo: Transrail, nlogo: No logo.

Prepared at: BS: Bescot, CD: Crewe Diesel, CF: Cardiff Canton, DR: Doncaster, EH: Eastleigh, ML: Motherwell, OC: Old Oak Common, TE: Thornaby, TO: Toton, XX: Unknown.

Beaucoup de Class 37s, Eurre, 12 June 2000. 37071, 37162, 37010 and 37376 head four long lines of British traction. Only 37888 was missing, having been purloined for a local village open day at St.Rambert d'Albon.

37100, Eurre, 15 October 1999.

37221, Eurre, 14 June 2000.

37073, 37686 and 37515, Eurre, 12 June 2000. Line-up of 'demic' locomotives, all subsequently returning to the UK without further use in France.

37888, St.Rambert D'Albon, 12 June 2000. A Class 37 at a local French village open day! 37888 managed to find employment in both France and Spain, although accident damage in Spain prevented a final return to the UK.

37170 and 37073, LGV Méditerranée Km499, 15 October 1999. Engineers' train.

37693 and 37803, LGV Méditerranée Km502, 15 October 1999. Ballast train with 37077 and 37261 at the rear.

37100 and 37077, Les Granges-Gontardes, 13 June 2000. Engineers' train.

37894, 37708 and 37696, Ile Vielle 14 June 2000. Ballast train with 37010 and 37037 at the rear.

4. Spain: Class 37s

After preparation at Toton and Thornaby depots, EWS moved fourteen heavy-weight Class 37/7s to Spain (via the Channel Tunnel) for use on construction work on a major section of the AVE (Alta Velocidad Española) Madrid-Barcelona line in 2001. The locomotives were hired by Continental Rail, a subcontractor to GIF (Gestor de Infraestructuras Ferroviarias), the body with overall responsibility for the construction of new high-speed lines in Spain.

The fourteen Class 37s were initially contracted to operate from two bases at Salilas de Jalón and Calatyud. However, over the ensuing years, the Class 37s moved steadily east towards Barcelona and ultimately on towards Girona, Figueres and the French border, progressively working on new contracts and being variously based at Puigverd de Lleida, Alcover, Vilafranca del Penedès, Hostalric and Llers. It should be noted that not all Class 37s worked on all contracts.

Whilst the bases were the main engineering and maintenance locations, in reality, the Class 37s, particularly when working ballast trains, operated for relatively long periods from remote 'virtual quarry' ballast dumps spaced at short intervals along the 'trace'. This method of operation was distinctly different from the prevailing French LGV-style, where trains were brought direct from the quarry to the LGV bases and then straight onto the 'trace' for discharge. This was possible in France where only one track gauge was involved; however in Spain the 'classic' lines are Iberian-gauge (1668mm) and the new AVE lines 'standard'-gauge (1435mm). The Spanish solution was to bring ballast to line-side dumps by road (or occasionally by train to mega dumps, followed by road distribution to smaller line-side dumps) with shovels loading ballast from the dump stock onto the rail wagons for movement to the required location on the 'trace' for discharging. Another difference in Spain was that a significant amount of ballast was laid on the 'trace' by road vehicles prior to the laying of the sleepers and rails, leaving only a relatively small amount of ballast for final delivery by rail.

The Spanish bases were generally positioned where existing Iberian-gauge tracks and the impending AVE route juxtaposed, to allow long-welded rails to be brought in on 'classic' rail wagons followed by transhipment onto 'standard'-gauge wagons, usually via intermediate storage.

Although the Class 37 fleet eventually spent over eleven years in Spain, in reality, locomotives spent extended periods of time out of traffic awaiting the commencement of the next contract (usually dictated by political and/or financial considerations) or waiting for preparatory infrastructure work to be completed prior to starting the tracklaying and final ballasting.

Details of the contracts worked by the Class 37s are given below.

The **Calatyud** (221km east of Madrid) and **Salilas de Jalón** (c255km from Madrid) contracts were adjacent to each other and when the tracks were joined, the previously separate fleets of Class 37s (seven at each base) were operated as one fleet from Calatyud and the Salillas base was returned to nature. The Calatyud/Salillas contracts ran roughly from Aguilar de Montuenga/Chaorna (170km from Madrid) in the west to

Zaragoza in the east (including Zaragoza-Delicias station (c305km from Madrid) and also a significant part of the high-speed city by-pass line, which may well explain the sighting of 37888 on ballast duties at the **La Cartuja** base (east of Zaragoza) during April 2003.

By mid-2003, work had largely been completed and the Class 37s were parked up at Calatyud awaiting developments. 37802/85/99 were early collision/derailment casualties and only ever saw service from Calatyud and Salillas de Jalón.

37718 was deployed on the Zaragoza to Huesca high-speed branch (via Zuera and Tardienta) between February and June 2003. The line to Huesca was inaugurated on 23 December 2003.

It is believed that the Class 37s had no involvement with tracklaying and ballasting work between Zaragoza (east) and Lleida (453km from Madrid).

The next and very significant tranche of work for the remaining eleven Class 37s involved construction from east of Lleida right through to the Llobregat valley immediately west of Barcelona, Barcelona itself being 621km from Madrid. The bases from which the Class 37s operated were **Puigverd de Lleida** (c465km east of Madrid), **Alcover** (c520km) and **Vilafranca del Penedès** (c575km), with major sub-bases at Camp de Tarragona (Perafort) and L'Arboç, both between Alcover and Vilafranca del Penedès. Despite the apparently long section of construction work, it was in reality sub-divided into a number of distinct contracts.

By February 2004, the eleven operational Class 37s had congregated at Puigverd de Lleida presumably being transferred in by rail. The Puigverd de Lleida and Alcover operations commenced as separate entities necessitating the transfer of the Alcover contingent by road from Puigverd de Lleida. 37714/6/8/99 and 37800/1 are known to have operated initially from Alcover, and 37702/3 and 37884/8 from Puigverd de Lleida; the initial deployment location of 37883 is unknown. Work had certainly commenced from these two bases by Spring 2004 and continued until at least February 2006, at which point the Puigverd de Lleida and Alcover sections became joined up. The Puigverd de Lleida base was seeing minimal use by May 2006 (other than for the storage of 37702 and 37888) and Alcover had been completely deserted by July 2006 and the site was awaiting redevelopment.

Work continued eastwards with the Class 37s operating from Perafort (Camp de Tarragona station) and L'Arboç with concentrated work upto the western outskirts of Vilafranca del Penedès underway upto about August/September 2006. 37716 is known to have continued work in this area on its own upto at least December 2006.

As work ran out on this section, the Class 37s returned west to the Puigverd de Lleida base for storage pending developments, with six locomotives stored there on 16 September 2006 (including 37718 and 37801, plus 'withdrawn' 37702 and 37888), and seven locomotives on 5 March and 17 May 2007 (37714/6/8, 37801/84, plus 37702 and 37888 on both dates). The 'withdrawn' pair were believed to have been scrapped in July 2009.

The next piece of work was eastwards from Vilafranca del Penedès through to the outskirts of Barcelona. However major civil engineering work in the Vilafranca del Penedès station area had necessitated the previous transfer of four recently externally refurbished Class 37s (37703/99, 37800/83) by road in February 2006; these four locomotives were brought in from Alcover by rail on 20-21 February 2006 to a point immediately west of Vilafranca del Penedès, and then moved the short distance by road to the base located just east of the city. Subsequent clearance of the Vilafranca del Penedès station 'blockage' enabled the five serviceable Class 37s stored at Puigverd de Lleida (37714/6/8, 37801/84) to be moved to the Vilafranca base sometime during the May-July 2007 period.

Work was insufficient for the available Class 37s, particularly when the fleet size here reached nine locomotives in mid-2007. Due to significant difficulties and consequent delays with building the AVE line through Barcelona city centre, work at the Vilafranca base through 2006-8 was inevitably somewhat pedestrian to say the least, with no work at all undertaken during the July-December 2008 period.

During their protracted stay in Vilafranca, three Class 37s (37799, 37801/83) fell into an unserviceable status and never worked again in Spain.

In January/February 2008 three locomotives (37703/16, 37884) were moved by road to the **Llers** base (near Figueres) to work on a separate contract between Figueres Els Hostelets and Perpignan (France), totalling circa 45km, although whether the Class 37s worked beyond the border town of Le Perthus (approximately 20km from Figueres) and on into France is unknown.

In March 2009, the remaining three serviceable Class 37s at Vilafranca del Penedès (37714/8, 37800) were moved by road to **Hostalric** for another construction contract, this time between Mollet (east of Barcelona) upto a point south of Girona. 37703/16, 37884 joined them at Hostalric in December 2008/January 2009, another road transfer, on completion of the work from Llers. Work on the Hostalric contract was rapid throughout 2009 with completion by May 2010. With the completion of this contract, the work of the Class 37s in Spain was done and all that was left for the final operational six was the long trip back to the UK. The three unserviceable Class 37s left stranded at Vilafranca del Penedès (37799, 37801/83) were finally scrapped in November 2011.

For completeness, it should be noted that the Class 37s were not involved in any work within the immediate area of Barcelona, or on the final 41km piece of AVE Madrid-Perpignan line construction between Girona and Figueres.

Over the eleven years that the Class 37s spent in Spain, accidents and fair wear-and-tear took their toll on the locomotives and ultimately only the Hostalric six returned to the UK in August 2012, the remainder (37702/99, 37801/2/83/5/8/99) being disposed of in Spain. Thus, in December 2011, 37703/14/6/8, 37800/84 left Hostalric (after over 18 months in store there) and moved to the Perpignan St.Charles Faisceau International Terminal in France for another eight months storage. On 8-9 August 2012 the six Class 37s were hauled from Perpignan to Valenton (south of Paris) via Nimes,

Lyon and Dijon by ECR Class 66 66203; onward movement to Calais Fréthun via Boulogne was undertaken on 10 August 2012. Transfer through the Channel Tunnel back to the UK took place for 37714, 37800/84 on 13 August and for 37703/16/8 on 29 August.

The various sections of the AVE Madrid-Perpignan line were inaugurated as follows: Madrid Atocha-Zaragoza-Lleida: 10 October 2003; Lleida-Camp de Tarragona: 18 December 2006; Camp de Tarragona-Barcelona Sants: 20 February 2008; Barcelona Sants-Figueres Vilafant: 8 January 2013 (although the Mollet (Barcelona)-Girona section had been completed in Autumn 2010), and the Figueres-Perpignan section in February 2009.

The Spanish Class 37s were repainted in the GIF light blue scheme with a broad dark blue bodyside band prior to departure from the UK. Continental Rail L-series numbers were applied to the Class 37s. Eight locomotives were renumbered prior to departure from the UK (L023-L025 and L030-L034). The numbering of the remaining six was left until the locomotives arrived in Spain. In the event, the fleet took up the number series L21-L34 (essentially in order of arrival at the two initial bases), necessitating the renumbering of the eight locomotives previously numbered in the L0xx series. When GIF metamorphosed into ADIF (Administrador de Infraestructuras Ferroviaria) on 1 January 2005, the locomotives lost their bodyside GIF lettering.

At the request of Continental Rail, all Class 37s were modified with wing-mirrors and cab air-conditioning equipment on arrival in Spain. The Spanish authorities were unimpressed by the poor UK-style headlights, so additional nose-top mounted headlights were fitted from about July 2002 and, therefore, early-withdrawn 37802/85/99 never carried this modification. During late-2005/early-2006, five locomotives (37703/99, 37800/83/8) were externally spruced-up and repainted at Alcover and Puigverd de Lleida as part of their preparation for the Vilafranca del Penedès contract commencing February 2006; however, collision damage to 37888 in late 2005 precluded its movement east.

Summary:-

Loco. No.	GIF No.	Orig GIF No.	Prep At	Date Ex-UK	Date loaded Irun	First Base & Date Arrived	Date Returned UK	Liveries/logos	Details	Refurbishment Base (Date)
37702	L30	------	TO	19/07/01	23/07/01	Salillas 25/07/01	–	GIF GIFlogo GIF nlogo	Blue CWB	–

Alternator failure; subsequently repaired under Bedale Railway Engines Ltd (BREL) ownership.
Sold to BREL, xx/01/07; unsold by administrators after BREL went into liquidation in xx/03/08.
C/U Puigverd de Lleida xx/07/09 (by Continental Rail). Disposal not proven.

Loco. No.	GIF No.	Orig GIF No.	Prep At	Date Ex-UK	Date loaded Irun	First Base & Date Arrived	Date Returned UK	Liveries/logos	Details	Refurbishment Base (Date)
37703	L25	L023	TE	29/05/01	05/06/01	Calatyud 07/06/01	29/08/12	GIF GIFlogo GIF nlogo	Black CWB	Puigverd de Lleida (noted ex-works 20/02/06)

Lifted onto low-loader at Vilafranca del Penedès (west) and off-loaded at Vilafranca base 21/02/06.
Lifted onto low-loader at Vilafranca del Penedès base 10/01/08 (prior to movement to Llers).
Noted en route from Perpignan to UK between Rivesaltes and Salses le Château on 08/08/12.

Loco. No.	GIF No.	Orig GIF No.	Prep At	Date Ex-UK	Date loaded Irun	First Base & Date Arrived	Date Returned UK	Liveries/logos	Details	Refurbishment Base (Date)
37714	L26	L031	TO	29/05/01	08/06/01	Calatyud 13/06/01	12/08/12	GIF GIFlogo GIF nlogo	Blue CWB	–

Lifted onto low-loader at Puigverd de Lleida 01/03/04. Arrived Alcover same day.
Lifted onto low-loader at Vilafranca del Penedès 17/03/09 and off-loaded at Hostalric 19/03/09.
Noted en route from Perpignan to UK between Rivesaltes and Salses le Château on 08/08/12.

Loco. No.	GIF No.	Orig GIF No.	Prep At	Date Ex-UK	Date loaded Irun	First Base & Date Arrived	Date Returned UK	Liveries/logos	Details	Refurbishment Base (Date)
37716	L23	L034	TO	23/05/01	28/05/01	Salillas 30/05/01	29/08/12	GIF GIFlogo GIF nlogo	Blue CWB	–

Noted on low-loader at Puigverd de Lleida 02/03/04, awaiting transfer to Alcover.
Lifted onto low-loader at Vilafranca del Penedès base 15/01/08 and off-loaded at Llers 17/01/08.
Noted en route from Perpignan to UK between Rivesaltes and Salses le Château on 08/08/12.

Loco. No.	GIF No.	Orig GIF No.	Prep At	Date Ex-UK	Date loaded Irun	First Base & Date Arrived	Date Returned UK	Liveries/logos	Details	Refurbishment Base (Date)
37718	L22	------	TO	18/04/01	30/04/01	Salillas 02/05/01	29/08/12	GIF GIFlogo GIF nlogo	Blue CWB	–

Moved by low-loader from Salillas to Osera (east of Zaragoza), then light engine to Lleida 09/07/01. Lifted onto low-loader at Osera 01/02/02, off-loaded at Salillas 02/02/02.
Lifted onto low-loader at Miraflores (Cartuja Baja) 13/02/03; off-loaded at Huesca 14/02/03. Moved by low-loader from Miraflores to Zaragoza 13/06/03.
Noted arriving and being off-loaded from low-loader at Alcover 27/02/04.
Due to be loaded onto low-loader at Vilafranca del Penedès 23/03/09, ready for movement to Hostalric.
Noted en route from Perpignan to UK between Rivesaltes and Salses le Château on 08/08/12.

Loco. No.	GIF No.	Orig GIF No.	Prep At	Date Ex-UK	Date loaded Irun	First Base & Date Arrived	Date Returned UK	Liveries/logos	Details	Refurbishment Base (Date)
37799	L27	L030	TO	07/06/01	19/06/01	Calatyud 21/06/01	–	GIF GIFlogo GIF nlogo	Blue CWB	Alcover (noted ex-works 21/07/05)

Off-loaded from low-loader at Alcover 01/03/04.
Lifted onto low-loader at Vilafranca del Penedès (west) and off-loaded at Vilafranca base 22/02/06.
Stored unserviceable at Vilafranca del Penedès, c2007. Sold Sandbach Car & Commercial, c12/08. Resold to Celsa Group, Barcelona.
C/U: Celsa Group at Vilafranca del Penedès, xx/11/11.

Loco. No.	GIF No.	Orig GIF No.	Prep At	Date Ex-UK	Date loaded Irun	First Base & Date Arrived	Date Returned UK	Liveries/logos	Details	Refurbishment Base (Date)
37800	L33	L025	TE	21/08/01	28/08/01	Salillas 30/08/01	12/08/12	GIF GIFlogo GIF nlogo	Black CWB	Alcover (noted ex-works 17/06/05)

Noted en route from Irun to Salillas de Jalon 29/08/01.
Noted on low-loader at Puigverd de Lleida 02/03/04, awaiting transfer to Alcover.
Lifted onto low-loader at Vilafranca del Penedès (west) 22/02/06 and off-loaded at Vilafranca base 23/02/06.
Noted on Vilafranca del Penedès base 31/07/07 with minor cab roof damage; subsequently repaired (new windows/horns, etc).
Lifted onto low-loader at Vilafranca del Penedès 17/03/09 and off-loaded at Hostalric 19/03/09.
Noted en route from Perpignan to UK between Rivesaltes and Salses le Château on 08/08/12.

Loco. No.	GIF No.	Orig GIF No.	Prep At	Date Ex-UK	Date loaded Irun	First Base & Date Arrived	Date Returned UK	Liveries/logos	Details	Refurbishment Base (Date)
37801	L29	L032	TO	10/07/01	18/07/01	Calatyud 20/07/01	–	GIF GIFlogo GIF nlogo	Blue CWB	–

Noted arriving and being off-loaded from low-loader at Alcover 27/02/04.
Stored unserviceable at Vilafranca del Penedès, c2007. Sold Sandbach Car & Commercial, c12/08. Resold to Celsa Group, Barcelona.
C/U: Celsa Group at Vilafranca del Penedès, xx/11/11.

Loco. No.	GIF No.	Orig GIF No.	Prep At	Date Ex-UK	Date loaded Irun	First Base & Date Arrived	Date Returned UK	Liveries/logos	Details	Refurbishment Base (Date)
37802	L32	------	TO	19/07/01	23/08/01	Calatyud 27/08/01	–	GIF GIFlogo	Blue CWB	–

Collision with track machine: Ateca, xx/07/02. Noted in process of being re-railed 11-13/07/02.
Noted at Calatyud 22/07/03 with engine/bogies/fuel tanks removed. C/U: Calatyud, 22-25/07/03.

Loco. No.	GIF No.	Orig GIF No.	Prep At	Date Ex-UK	Date loaded Irun	First Base & Date Arrived	Date Returned UK	Liveries/logos	Details	Refurbishment Base (Date)
37883	L28	------	TO	10/07/01	xx/07/01	Calatyud 17/07/01	–	GIF GIFlogo gifl nlogo	Blue CWB	Puigverd de Lleida (noted ex-works by 20/02/06)

Off-loaded from low-loader at Vilafranca del Penedès base 22/02/06.
Stored unserviceable at Vilafranca del Penedès, c2007. Believed sold to Sandbach Car & Commercial, date unknown. Resold to Celsa Group, Barcelona.
C/U: Celsa Group at Vilafranca del Penedès, xx/11/11.

Loco. No.	GIF No.	Orig GIF No.	Prep At	Date Ex-UK	Date loaded Irun	First Base & Date Arrived	Date Returned UK	Liveries/logos	Details	Refurbishment Base (Date)
37884	L34	------	TO	21/08/01	05/09/01	Calatyud 07/09/01	12/08/12	GIF GIFlogo GIF nlogo	Blue CWB	–

Lifted onto low-loader at Vilafranca del Penedès base 22/01/08 and off-loaded at Llers 04/02/08.
Departed Llers 13/01/09 and moved to Hostalric. Loaded onto low-loader in December 2008; departure delayed by bad weather.
Noted en route from Perpignan to UK between Rivesaltes and Salses le Château on 08/08/12.

Loco. No.	GIF No.	Orig GIF No.	Prep At	Date Ex-UK	Date loaded Irun	First Base & Date Arrived	Date Returned UK	Liveries/logos	Details	Refurbishment Base (Date)
37885	L24	L033	TO	23/05/01	31/05/01	Salillas 04/06/01	–	GIF GIFlogo	Blue/Black CWB	–

Noted Irun Kostorbe on 29/05/01.
Derailment/accident damage: Zaragoza, 27/02/02 (with 37899). Removed from bogies at Zaragoza 28/03/02.
C/U: Vias Y Construcciones, Fuenlabrada, Madrid, xx/07/03.

Loco. No.	GIF No.	Orig GIF No.	Prep At	Date Ex-UK	Date loaded Irun	First Base & Date Arrived	Date Returned UK	Liveries/logos	Details	Refurbishment Base (Date)
37888	L31	L024	TE	23/07/01	26/07/01	Salillas 31/07/01	–	GIF GIFlogo GIF nlogo	Black CWB	Puigverd de Lleida (noted ex-works 06/06/05)

Collision with track machine, damage to No.1 cab end, between July and November 2005.
Sold to Bedale Railway Engines Ltd xx/01/07; unsold by administrators after BREL went into liquidation in xx/03/08.
C/U Puigverd de Lleida xx/07/09 (by Continental Rail). Disposal not proven.

Loco. No.	GIF No.	Orig GIF No.	Prep At	Date Ex-UK	Date loaded Irun	First Base & Date Arrived	Date Returned UK	Liveries/logos	Details	Refurbishment Base (Date)
37899	L21	------	TE	18/04/01	23/04/01	Salillas 25/04/01	–	GIF GIFlogo	Black CWB	–

Derailment/accident damage: Zaragoza, 27/02/02 (with 37885). Removed from bogies at Zaragoza 28/03/02.
C/U: Vias Y Construcciones, Fuenlabrada, Madrid, xx/07/03.

Abbreviations:

Prepared at:	TE: Thornaby, TO: Toton.
Livery:	nlogo: No logos.
Details:	CWB: Front cab window beading.
Notes:	C/U: Cut-up.

37888 (L024), Thornaby TMD, 12 June 2001. Prepared for movement to Spain, complete with L024 identifier. On arrival in Spain, the L024 number was superceded by L31. Note the black rubber front cab window beading, which immediately distinguished the locomotives prepared at Thornaby compared with those at Toton where the beading was painted light-blue to match the main livery.

37800 (L33) and 37703 (L25), Location unknown, 19 February 2002. *(Keith Butler)*

37899 (L21) and 37885 (L24), Zaragoza, 27 March 2002. Run-away accident with both locomotives subsequently written-off for scrap. *(Keith Butler)*

37885 (L24) and 37899 (L21), Zaragoza, 28 March 2002. In the process of bogie removal prior to movement to the Vias Y Construcciones site at Fuenlabrada, Madrid, for storage. *(Keith Butler)*

37884 (L34) and 37716 (L23), Calatyud Base, 21 May 2002. The high-speed lines are immediately behind 37884, with the 'classic' lines just beyond.

37703 (L25) and 37799 (L27), Feria de Muestras, 19 May 2002. Two Class 37s on a rake of mixed hoppers used to ferry ballast from the various 'virtual quarry' dumps, positioned about 10-15km apart along the 'trace', to the drop sites.

Above left: 37802 (L32), Ateca, 12 July 2002. Following collision with a track machine and subsequent derailment on a viaduct near Ateca. *(Keith Butler)*

Above right: 37802 (L32), Ateca, 11 July 2002. *(Keith Butler)*

Below left: 37802 (L32), Ateca, 13 July 2002. Recovery work in progress with assistance from three Class 37s including 37801 (L29). *(Keith Butler)*

Below right: 37802 (L32), Ateca, 13 July 2002. Subsequently written-off for scrap. *(Keith Butler)*

37801 (L29), Chaorne, 20 May 2002. Another ballast dump with wagons being loaded by mechanical shovels.

37718 (L22), Cabolafuente, 20 May 2002. Six heavily-loaded ballast hoppers being transferred from the Cabolafuente 'virtual quarry' to the drop-site several kilometres along the 'trace'.

Above left: **37799 (L27) and 58041 (L36), Montagut/Raimat, 23 February 2004.** A relatively rare sight of a Class 37 and Class 58 together in Spain. *(Keith Butler)*

Above right: **58043 (L37), 37702 (L30), 37883 (L28) or 37884 (L34), 37703 (L25) on the left, together with 37714 (L26), 37716 (L23), 37800 (L33) and 37799 (L27) and on the right, Puigverd de Lleida, 24 February 2004.** The four Class 37s on the right were queued up awaiting transfer by road to Alcover base. *(Keith Butler)*

Above left: **37718 (L22) and 37801 (L29), Alcover, 27 February 2004.** Two Class 37s arriving at the Alcover base following road transfer from Puigverd de Lleida. *(Keith Butler)*

Above right: **37714 (L26), Puigverd de Lleida, 1 March 2004.** Loading onto road transport for movement to Alcover. *(Keith Butler)*

Below left: **37703 (L25) and 37702 (L30), plus 37888 (L31) and either 37883 (L28) or 37884 (L34) on a rail train, Puigverd de Lleida, 1 March 2004.** *(Keith Butler)*

Below right: **37800 (L33) and 37716 (L23), Puigverd de Lleida, 2 March 2004.** On low-loaders ready for movement to Alcover. *(Keith Butler)*

37888 (L31) and 37702 (L30), Alcover Base, 20 February 2006. 37888 (accident-damaged) and 37702 (requiring electrical repairs) are positioned nearest to the camera. Beyond are the repainted 37703/99, 37800/83 awaiting their rail and road move to Vilafranca del Penedès; but for the accident damage, 37888 would also have been a contender for movement to Vilafranca having also received cosmetic treatment.

(Keith Harper)

37800 (L33), Vilafranca del Penedès Base, 23 February 2006. 37800 being lifted off a low-loader after road transportation was required to bridge the engineering gap in the Vilafranca station area. *(Keith Harper)*

37716 (L23) and 37718 (L22), La Riba Viaduct, 11 May 2006. Strain-gauge testing. *(Keith Harper)*

37888 (L31) and 37702 (L30), Puigverd de Lleida Base, 3 July 2006. Both locomotives lie out of use, never to work again.

37883 (L28), Vilafranca del Penedès Base, 3 July 2006. 37883 positioned under the rail gantries used to tranship long rails from Iberian-gauge wagons onto standard-gauge wagons (frequently via intermediate storage).

37703 (L25) and 37799 (L27), Vilafranca del Penedès Base, 3 July 2006. Two refurbished Class 37s awaiting their next turn of duty. White wheel-rims and bogie footsteps distinguished the five refurbished locomotives.

37716 (L23), 37718 (L22) and 37884 (L34), L'Arboç, 3 July 2006. In amongst the vineyards, three Class 37s idle away a few hours before further ballast train duties.

37716 (L23), Perafort 14 December 2006. Ancient and modern in the Camp de Tarragona station! *(Keith Harper)*

37718 (L22), 37884 (L34), 37716 (L23), 37714 (L26), 37801 (L29), 37702 (L30), 37888 (L31), Puigverd de Lleida Base, 5 March 2007.
Temporarily stored awaiting further developments. *(Keith Harper)*

37884 (L34), Vilafranca del Penedès, 30 July 2007. 37884 starting-up underneath the rail transhipment gantry.

37884 (L34), Llers, 4 February 2008. 37884 being off-loaded from a road trailer after movement from Vilafranca del Penedès, ready for deployment on the Llers contract towards the French border which it shared with 37703 and 37716. *(Keith Harper)*

37714 (L26), Hostalric, 19 March 2009. 37714 being off-loaded from a road trailer after movement from Vilafranca del Penedès. Hostalric was the last operational base for the Class 37s. *(Keith Harper)*

37884 (L34) and 37718 (L22), Hostalric, 30 April 2009. 37884 and 37718 stabled immediately adjacent to the recently constructed high-speed line connecting Barcelona and Perpignan (France).

37703 (L25) and 37800 (L33), Santa Maria de Palautordera, 30 April 2009. Operating from the Hostalric base, 37703 and 37800 are seen topping and tailing a long rake of ballast wagons.

37703 (L25) and 37800 (L33), Santa Maria de Palautordera, 30 April 2009. Both locomotives were returned to the UK, with 37703 now owned by DRS albeit on loan to the Bo'ness & Kinneil Railway, and 37800 owned by Europhoenix and loaned to the Rail Operations Group.

37801 (L29), 37883 (L28) and 37799 (L27), Vilafranca del Penedès Base, 30 April 2009. Stored unserviceable at the time of this photograph, all three locomotives were subsequently sold and scrapped in Spain by the Celsa Group in 2011.

5. Italy: Class 37s

Italy was the home for two EWS Class 37s between July 2001 and March 2003. This pair was hired to the Italian consortium CEAAV (Consorzio Europeo Armamento Alta Velocita) and deployed on high-speed line construction work between Napoli and Rome. The locomotives were progressively based at **Capua** (north of Napoli), **Tora E Piccilli** and **Ceprano** (south of Rome).

Both locomotives carried the EWS maroon/gold livery and their UK numbers whilst in Italy.

Work was completed by mid-2002 and given the unlikelihood of further work were returned to the UK for further use in 2003.

Summary:-

Loco No.	Prepared at	Ex-UK	Returned UK	Liveries/logos
37893	**Eastleigh/Toton**	20/07/01	07/03/03	**EWS EWSlogo**
37895	**Toton**	20/07/01	07/03/03	**EWS EW&Slogo**

37883 and 37895, near Modane, date unknown. En route to Italy with SNCF Class CC6500 406545 providing haulage. Many CC6500s were allocated to Vénissieux (Lyons) depot during the early 2000s and the train was probably en route from Lyons to Turin via the French border town Modane. *(Keith Butler)*

37895 and 37893, Italy, date unknown. *Traction* magazine (September 2001) indicates that 37895 was a last minute substitution for 37896.
(Keith Butler)

6. France: LGV Est Class 56s and 58s

The next major European high-speed construction project involving British traction was the LGV Est line in France between Vaires-sur-Marne (near Paris) and Baudrecourt (near Metz). Companies involved were Fertis (a subsidiary of VFLI, itself a subsidiary of SNCF), plus TSO (Travaux du Sud Ouest) and Seco (both private track maintenance firms). Three operating bases were set up as follows:-

St.Hilaire base (149km from the start of the LGV at Vaires). Work started in the easterly direction for 71km upto and including the new Gare-Meuse station near Mondrecourt at km point 220. After this, track was laid 29km to the west, almost to the Gare Champagne-Ardennes to the south of Reims.

Ocquerre base (34km from Vaires, north-east of Meaux). Work started eastwards for 86km upto and including the Gare Champagne-Ardennes, to meet up with the track from St.Hilaire, then 34km westwards to Vaires where the new line met the classic Paris-Strasbourg main line.

Pagny-sur-Moselle (270km from Vaires, between Metz and Nancy) simultaneously started tracklaying westwards for 50km to meet track from St.Hilaire at Gare Meuse, then eastwards for 30km to the junctions with the Metz-Forbach/Strasbourg lines at Baudrecourt.

Unlike the LGV Méditerranée project, electrification catenary was erected prior to tracklaying and involved road transportation. The Class 56s and 58s were, therefore, predominantly involved with the movement of ballast, sleepers and rails.

The first nine Class 56s and fourteen Class 58s were moved through the Channel Tunnel to St.Hilaire during the period September to November 2004, with a further four Class 56s arriving in April/May 2005. As work drew to a close at St.Hilaire, the Class 56s and 58s there were redeployed at Ocquerre and Pagny-sur-Moselle. Seventeen additional Class 56s and five Class 58s were brought in to assist. In the end, forty-nine EWS locomotives (thirty Class 56s and nineteen Class 58s) operated on the LGV Est line.

By late January 2006, the three elements fused together into the full route, enabling the possibility of the Class 56s and 58s moving between Ocquerre and Pagny-sur-Moselle. This, indeed, they did as can be seen from the table below; it is entirely possible that some movements went unrecorded. However, on the basis of known information, only 56087, 58004/34 managed to work from all three LGV Est bases.

The locomotives were 'sectorised' and carried appropriate liveries to reflect their operators. Forty-one were operated by Fertis (predominantly for ballast trains), four by TSO and four by Seco (predominantly for tracklaying work), although towards the end they tended to become 'general-user' locomotives. As a consequence, most of the Class 58s lost their Seco/TSO decals. All locomotives returned to the UK via the Channel Tunnel.

During their time in France, the Class 56s and 58s were frequently beset by wheelset problems, usually caused by hand-brakes being left on on the rear locomotives during the evening return to base movements. Rectification was usually undertaken at nearby SNCF depots (for example, 56038 Thionville (January 2006), 56058 Paris Ourcq (May 2006), 56074 VFLI Loco Workshop, Petite Rosselle (February 2006)). Traction motor problems were also an issue, these being resolved through bogie swaps or depot repairs (for example, 56096 & 56105 Creutzwald (March 2006). 56091 returned to the UK briefly for camshaft repairs and tyre-turning.

Failure rates of locomotives at Ocquerre were significantly greater than those experienced at Pagny-sur-Moselle. This was attributed to the lower skill levels of the Ocquerre drivers recruited 'off the street', compared with the drivers at Pagny who had previous railway experience. However, the number of locomotives out of traffic at Ocquerre with wheelset and traction motor issues was such that several recently withdrawn SNCF 68000 and 68500 locomotives had to be drafted in. In addition, trains were reduced in size to reduce traction motor overheating.

Summary (Class 56):

Loco No.	Prepared at	Ex-UK	Operational Bases (including last or first dates noted)	Returned UK	Liveries/logos
56007	OC Operational pool (11/09/06).	01/09/05	Pagny-sur-Moselle	05/11/06	Fertis ½bws Fertislogo (lhc/b)
56018	TO Reserve pool (11/09/06).	04/05/05	St.Hilaire (last 31/08/05), Pagny-sur-Moselle (first 14/10/05)	27/01/07	Fertis bws Fertislogo (lhc/b)
56031	OC Operational pool (11/09/06).	28/06/05	Ocquerre	23/12/06	Fertis bws Fertislogo (lhc/b/rhc)
56032	TO Operational pool (11/09/06).	14/05/05	Ocquerre	30/10/06	Fertis bws Fertislogo (lhc/b)
56038	TO Operational pool (11/09/06).	07/10/04	St.Hilaire (last 28/07/05), Pagny-sur-Moselle (first 06/10/05)	27/12/06	Fertis bws Fertislogo (lhc/b)
56049	EH/BBH Withdrawn pool (11/09/06). Loose tyres.	26/05/05	Ocquerre	19/11/06	Fertis nbws Fertislogo (lhc/b/rhc)
56051	EH/BBH Operational pool (11/09/06).	22/06/05	Ocquerre	13/10/06	Fertis nbws Fertislogo (lhc/b/rhc) rhcn

Loco No.	Prepared at	Ex-UK	Operational Bases (including last or first dates noted)	Returned UK	Liveries/logos
56058	**TO**	**15/06/05**	**Ocquerre**	**15/10/06**	**Fertis bws Fertislogo (lhc/b)**
Withdrawn pool (11/09/06).					
56059	**TO**	**12/10/04**	**St.Hilaire (last 10/08/05), Pagny-sur-Moselle (first 06/10/05)**	**03/11/06**	**Fertis bws Fertislogo (lhc/b)**
Operational pool (11/09/06).					
56060	**TO**	**12/10/04**	**St.Hilaire (last 10/08/05), Ocquerre (first 31/08/05)**	**23/10/06**	**Fertis bws Fertislogo (lhc/b)**
Reserve pool (11/09/06).					
56065	**EH/BBH**	**26/05/05**	**Ocquerre**	**09/10/06**	**Fertis nbws Fertislogo (lhc/b/rhc)**
Withdrawn pool (110906).					
56069	**TO**	**30/09/04**	**St.Hilaire (last 27/07/05), Pagny-sur-Moselle (first 12/10/05)**	**11/01/07**	**Fertis bws Fertislogo (lhc/b)**
'Autorisation de Circulation' documentation dated 03/08/05 for movement from St.Hilaire to Pagny-sur-Moselle. Operational pool (11/09/06).					
56071	**OC/BBH**	**24/08/05**	**Pagny-sur-Moselle (last 17/11/05), Ocquerre (first 20/03/06)**	**03/11/06**	**Fertis nbws Fertislogo (lhc/b/rhc)**
Noted en route: Pérenchies, 31/08/05. Operational pool (11/09/06).					
56074	**OC**	**06/09/05**	**Pagny-sur-Moselle**	**25/10/06**	**Fertis ½bws Fertislogo (lhc/b/rhc)**
Reserve pool (11/09/06).					
56078	**TO**	**09/09/04**	**St.Hilaire (last 31/08/05), Pagny-sur-Moselle (first 16/11/05)**	**05/05/07**	**Fertis bws Fertislogo (lhc/b)**
Noted en route: Don Sainghin (Lille); 10/09/04, Freyming Merlebach, 28/09/04. 'Autorisation de Circulation' documentation dated 24/09/05 for movement from St.Hilaire to Pagny-sur-Moselle. Withdrawn pool (11/09/06). Wheelset flats.					
56081	**EH/BBH**	**01/07/05**	**Ocquerre**	**27/09/06**	**Fertis nbws Fertislogo (lhc/b)**
Withdrawn pool (11/09/06).					

Loco No.	Prepared at	Ex-UK	Operational Bases (including last or first dates noted)	Returned UK	Liveries/logos
56087	TO	05/10/04	St.Hilaire (last 19/10/05), Pagny-sur-Moselle (first 16/11/05, last 17/11/05),Ocquerre (first 20/03/06, last 25/04/06), Pagny-sur-Moselle (first 08/05/06)	25/01/07	Fertis bws Fertislogo (lhc/b)

'Autorisation de Circulation' documentation dated 27/10/05 for movement from St.Hilaire to Pagny-sur-Moselle.
Operational pool (11/09/06).

56090	BBH/TO	19/10/04	St.Hilaire (last 01/07/05), Ocquerre (first 21/07/05)	23/10/06	Fertis nbws Fertislogo (lhc/b/rhc)

Operational pool (11/09/06).

56091	TO OC/TM	23/06/05 03/05/06	Ocquerre (last 20/03/06), to UK for repairs, Pagny-sur-Moselle (first 08/05/06)	01/04/06 27/12/06	Fertis bws Fertislogo (lhc/b)

'Autorisation de Circulation' documentation dated 15/03/06 for movement from Ocquerre to Calais Fréthun.
Operational pool (11/09/06).

56094	OC/BBH	21/07/05	Ocquerre	04/12/06	Fertis nbws Fertislogo (lhc/b/rhc)

Operational pool (11/09/06).

56095	OC	12/07/05	Ocquerre	09/10/06	Fertis bws Fertislogo (lhc/b/rhc)

Withdrawn pool (11/09/06). Traction motors.

56096	TO	27/04/05	St.Hilaire (last 01/09/05), Pagny-sur-Moselle (first 16/11/05)	27/10/06	Fertis bws Fertislogo (lhc/b)

Withdrawn pool (11/09/06).

56103	OC	03/11/05	Pagny-sur-Moselle (last 13/07/06), Ocquerre (first 25/08/06)	17/11/06	Fertis ½bws Fertislogo (lhc/b)

Operational pool (11/09/06).

56104	BBH	21/10/05	Pagny-sur-Moselle	17/01/07	Fertis nbws Fertislogo (lhc/b/rhc)

Operational pool (11/09/06).

56105	TO	27/04/05	St.Hilaire (last 28/07/05), Pagny-sur-Moselle (first 12/10/05)	27/01/07	Fertis bws Fertislogo (lhc/b)

Withdrawn pool (11/09/06).

Loco No.	Prepared at	Ex-UK	Operational Bases (including last or first dates noted)	Returned UK	Liveries/logos
56106	**TO**	**04/05/05**	**St.Hilaire (last 01/07/05), Ocquerre (first 21/07/05)**	**24/06/07**	**Fertis bws Fertislogo (lhc/b)**
Withdrawn pool (11/09/06). Wheelset flats.					
56113	**OC**	**03/11/05**	**Pagny-sur-Moselle (last 17/11/05), Ocquerre (first 20/03/06, last 11/04/06), Pagny-sur-Moselle (first 08/05/06, last 09/07/06), Ocquerre (first 18/08/06)**	**15/10/06**	**Fertis ½bws Fertislogo (lhc/b)**
Operational pool (11/09/06).					
56115	**BBH/EH**	**04/11/05**	**Pagny-sur-Moselle (last 10/07/06), Ocquerre (first xx/xx/06)**	**01/12/06**	**Fertis nbws Fertislogo (lhc/b/rhc)**
Operational pool (11/09/06).					
56117	**BBH/TO**	**05/10/04**	**St.Hilaire (last 30/06/05), Ocquerre (first 21/07/05)**	**09/10/06**	**Fertis nbws Fertislogo (lhc/b)**
Reserve pool (11/09/06).					
56118	**BBH/TO**	**30/09/04**	**St.Hilaire (last 01/07/05), Ocquerre (first 21/07/05)**	**07/06/06**	**Fertis nbws Fertislogo (lhc/b)**
Fire damaged on 18/11/05 on trace. Returned early to UK.					

Summary (Class 58):

Loco No.	Prepared at	Ex-UK	Operational Bases (including last or first dates noted)	Returned UK	Liveries/logos
58004	TO	15/10/04	St.Hilaire (last 19/10/05), Pagny-sur-Moselle (first 16/11/05, last 12/07/06), Oquerre (first xx/xx/06)	15/09/06	Fertis Fertislogo (lhc/b)

Withdrawn pool (11/09/06).

58007	TO	14/10/04	St.Hilaire (last 22/08/05), Pagny-sur-Moselle (first 16/11/05)	27/10/06	Seco Secologo (rhc) (logos subsequently removed)

Noted en route: Châlon (Reims), 21/10/04.
Withdrawn pool (11/09/06).

58009	TO	03/11/04	St.Hilaire (last 10/08/05), Pagny-sur-Moselle (first 14/10/05)	17/01/07	Seco Secologo (rhc) (logos subsequently removed)

Operational pool (11/09/06).

58010	EH	23/06/05	Ocquerre	01/12/06	Fertis Fertislogo (lhc/b/rhc)

Withdrawn pool (11/09/06). Wheelset flats.

58011	EH	30/06/05	Ocquerre	11/10/06	Fertis Fertislogo (lhc/b/rhc)

Withdrawn pool (11/09/06).

58015	EH/TM	07/10/04	St.Hilaire (last 28/07/05), Pagny-sur-Moselle (first 31/08/05)	17/01/07	Fertis Fertislogo (lhc/b)

Operational pool (11/09/06).

58016	EH	14/05/05	Ocquerre	25/05/06	Fertis Fertislogo (lhc/b/rhc)

Alternator damage 30/01/06. Bogies relinquished to 58021 in April 2006 prior to early return to UK.

58018	EH	23/08/05	Ocquerre	06/12/06	Fertis Fertislogo (lhc/b/rhc)

Withdrawn pool (11/09/06). Wheelset flats.

58021	EH	13/07/05	Ocquerre	16/11/06	Fertis Fertislogo (lhc/b/rhc)

Bogies from 58016 during April 2006 following wheelset damage.
Operational pool (11/09/06).

58027	TO	21/10/04	St.Hilaire (last 21/07/05), Pagny-sur-Moselle (first 04/08/05)	02/11/06	Seco Secologo (rhc) (logos subsequently removed)

'Autorisation de Circulation' documentation dated 22/07/05 for movement from St.Hilaire to Pagny-sur-Moselle.
Withdrawn pool (11/09/06).

Loco No.	Prepared at	Ex-UK	Operational Bases (including last or first dates noted)	Returned UK	Liveries/logos
58032	**TO**	**19/10/04**	**St.Hilaire (last 01/09/05), Pagny-sur-Moselle (first 06/10/05)**	**27/12/06**	**Fertis Fertislogo (lhc/b)**

Operational pool (11/09/06).

58033	**OC/EH/OC**	**28/10/04**	**St.Hilaire (last 19/07/05), Pagny-sur-Moselle (first 04/08/05)**	**12/08/06**	**TSO TSOlogo (lhc/rhc/f) (logos subsequently removed)**

'Autorisation de Circulation' documentation dated 22/07/05 for movement from St.Hilaire to Pagny-sur-Moselle.

58034	**EH/TM**	**21/10/04**	**St.Hilaire (last 19/10/05), Pagny-sur-Moselle (first 16/11/05, last 17/11/05),Ocquerre (first 20/03/06)**	**24/11/06**	**Fertis Fertislogo (lhc/b)**

Withdrawn pool (11/09/06). Wheelset flats; last day in service 20/03/06?

58035	**TO**	**27/10/04**	**St.Hilaire (last 31/08/05), Pagny-sur-Moselle (first 06/10/05)**	**05/05/07**	**Fertis Fertislogo (lhc/b)**

'Autorisation de Circulation' documentation dated 20/09/05 for movement from St.Hilaire to Pagny-sur-Moselle.
Withdrawn pool (11/09/06). Wheelset flats.

58040	**TO**	**13/11/04**	**St.Hilaire (last 10/08/05), Pagny-sur-Moselle (first 06/10/05)**	**12/08/06**	**Seco Secologo (rhc) (logos retained)**

58046	**TO**	**09/09/04**	**St.Hilaire (last 10/08/05), Pagny-sur-Moselle (first 06/10/05)**	**24/01/07**	**Fertis Fertislogo (lhc/b)**

Noted en route: Don Sainghin (Lille); 10/09/04, Freyming Merlebach, 28/09/04.
Operational pool on 11/09/06.

58047	**OC/EH/TO**	**28/10/04**	**St.Hilaire (last 10/08/05), Pagny-sur-Moselle (first 12/10/05)**	**10/08/06**	**TSO TSOlogo (lhc/rhc/f) (logos subsequently removed)**

58049	**OC/TM**	**17/11/04**	**St.Hilaire (last 19/10/05), Pagny-sur-Moselle (first 16/11/05)**	**02/11/06**	**TSO TSOlogo (lhc/rhc/f) (logos subsequently removed)**

Noted en route: Nieppe, 20/11/04.
Operational pool on 110906.

58050	**OC/TM**	**17/11/04**	**St.Hilaire (last 21/07/05), Pagny-sur-Moselle (04/08/05)**	**26/10/06**	**TSO TSO logo (lhc/rhc/f) (logos subsequently removed)**

Noted en route: Nieppe, 20/11/04.
'Autorisation de Circulation' documentation dated 22/07/05 for movement from St.Hilaire to Pagny-sur-Moselle.
Withdrawn pool (11/09/06).

Abbreviations:-

Prepared at: BBH: Bristol Barton Hill, EH: Eastleigh, OC: Old Oak Common, TM: Temple Mills, TO: Toton.

Class 56 cab window surrounds: bws: black front & side cab window surrounds (TO painted locos, plus early OC repaints (56031/95)),
½bws: front cab windows only with black surrounds (later OC repaints),
nbws : no black window surrounds (BBH repaints).

Logo positions: lhc: left-hand cabside, rhc: right-hand cabside, b: bodyside, f: cab front.

Number position: rhcn (right-hand cabside number.

Additional Notes:

Seco/TSO Class 58 numbers were modified from 580xx to 58-0xx.
56078 and 58046 were initially delivered to VFLI, Petite-Rosselle for driver training.
Pagny-sur-Moselle operational fleet dropped from twelve to five locomotives from 30/09/06.

56105, 58032, 58009 and 56117, St.Hilaire, 3 May 2005. St.Hilaire was the first operational base used for the LGV Est (Phase 1) construction, located roughly mid-way between Paris and Metz.

56078 with 56069, plus 56059 and 58027, Pagny-sur-Moselle, 16 November 2005. Pagny-sur-Moselle was the base at the eastern end of the LGV trace, this base taking most of the locomotives from St.Hilaire when work was completed there.

56096 and 662418, Pagny-sur-Moselle, 17 November 2005.

56007, Pagny-sur-Moselle, 22 March 2006. Romanian-built!

56038 and 56091, Pagny-sur-Moselle, 19 September 2006. Note the proximity of the yard to the town of the same name; the early morning smoky starts from the Class 56s inevitably generated some complaints from the local populace!

58032, plus 58027, 56096, 58007, 58050, 56105 and 58035, Pagny-sur-Moselle, 19 September 2006.

662424 and 662502, plus 58021 and 56090, Ocquerre, 12 May 2006. Ocquerre base was located at the west end of the LGV Est trace. Both the Ocquerre and St.Hilaire sites returned to farmland after completion of construction work; only the yard at Pagny-sur-Moselle remains today, adjacent to the SNCF station.

58016, Ocquerre, 4 April 2006. After suffering electrical damage, 58016 relinquished its bogies to 58021; 58016 was subsequently returned to the UK without further use in France.

58050 and 58027, La Cheppe, 3 May 2005. 58050, together with 58033/47/9, carried the TSO yellow livery. Empty concrete sleeper wagons being returned to St.Hilaire base.

58007, Tilloy-et-Bellay, 4 May 2005. 58007 along with 58009/27/40 carried the orange and yellow Seco Rail livery whilst working on the LGV Est contract. At this time 58007 was operating from the St.Hilaire base.

58007 and 58050, alongside 58035 and 56096, Buoy, 20 July 2005.

58032 and 58046, with 56105 and 58015, Vigneulles, 16 November 2005. Fertis livery.

56115 and 56103, plus 56113 and 56087, Tautecourt, 17 November 2005.

56117 and 56032, plus 58011 and 56095, Trugny, 18 November 2005.

58034 and 56087 stand face-to-face with 58011 and 56049, Vrigny, 20 March 2006. Operating from the Ocquerre base, two mixed Class 56/58 pairings are seen on ballast trains near Vrigny.

56031 and 56060 side-by-side with 58034 and 56087, Vrigny, 20 March 2006.

58027, Pagny-sur-Moselle, 23 March 2006. 58027 in Seco Rail livery is seen departing from the base with a rake of ballast wagons, with 58047 and 58050 bringing up the rear.

56031 and 56032, plus SNCF 668504 and 668512, Iverny, 11 May 2006. 56031 and 56032 on a rake of ballast hoppers with SNCF assistance.

56071 and 56117, with 56095 and 56094, Charny, 11 May 2006.

56071 and 56117, with 56095 and 56094, Ocquerre Viaduct, 11 May 2006. Part of the Ocquerre base can be seen in the valley below, illustrating the severe climb for locomotives hauling loaded ballast trains out of the base early each weekday morning.

56081 and 56051, with SNCF 468081 and 668531, Barcy, 12 May 2006.

7. Netherlands: ACTS Class 58s

From 2003, EWS hired three otherwise redundant Class 58s to Dutch private operator ACTS (Afzet Container Transport Systeem). Five locomotives were originally envisaged but only three actually migrated across the Channel. 58039 arrived in Holland in June 2003, followed by 58044 in October; 58038 subsequently arrived in May 2005. All were shipped via Immingham Docks. The Class 58s were deployed on container services, with a heavy concentration on the so-called 'Veendam Shuttles'.

The locomotives were prepared at Toton (including the fitting of modified light clusters), and renumbered 5811 (58039), 5812 (58044) and 5814 (58038); 5811 and 5812 were repainted into the ACTS blue and yellow scheme, whilst 5814 was repainted into Vos Logistics black and red colours.

ACTS ceased using the Class 58s in March 2009. Following repainting into the ETF yellow livery at the RET Kleiweg workshops at Rotterdam Hillgersberg Zuid (west of Rotterdam Noord station), the three locomotives were moved to Villersexel in France during July 2009 for use on the LGV Rhin-Rhône construction project (see Section 8).

Summary:-

ACTS No.	BR No.	Prepared at	Ex-UK	Commenced ACTS duties	Liveries/logos	Completed ACTS duties	Repainted for France	Moved NL to F
5811	58039	Toton	27/06/03	xx/09/03	ACTS ACTSlogo(b)	14/03/09	25/06/09-10/07/09	31/07/09
5812	58044	Toton	16/10/03	xx/10/03	ACTS ACTSlogo(b)	xx/03/09	05/06/09-25/06/09	31/07/09
		Noted on road trailer at Rotterdam Docks on 17/10/03.						
5814	58038	Toton	07/05/05	xx/05/05	VOS Logistics VOSlogo(b/f)/ACTS logo(lhc/rhc)	xx/02/09	12/05/09-05/06/09	31/07/09

Abbreviations:-

Logo positions: lhc: left-hand cabside, rhc: right-hand cabside, b: bodyside, f: cab front.

Additional notes:

Observations en route to France: Kijfhoek yard, Rotterdam (NL): 23/07/09+26/07/09, Dordrecht Suid (NL): 28/07/09 (transit), Antwerpen Noord (B): 29/07/09, XX (Antwerpen (B)-Monceau (B)): 29/07/09 (transit), XX (Monceau (B)-Somain (F)): 31/07/09 (transit).

58044(5812), Rotterdam Port, 17 October 2003. *(Keith Butler)*

58038 (5814), Zwolle, 6 July 2007. 5814 (58038) stabled inside the Nedtrain Zwolle depot awaiting attention prior to railtour duties the following day.

58038 (5814), Rotterdam CS, 7 July 2007. Mercia Charters 'That Which Survives' railtour.

58044 (5812) and 6703, Moordrecht, 19 June 2008. ACTS locomotives 5812 (58044) and 6703 pass Moordrecht on a rake of container wagons, one of the 'Veendam shuttles'. The difference between the loading gauges of the two locomotives is immediately apparent.

58038 (5814), Rotterdam Waalhaven, 19 June 2008. 5814 doing business with its staple diet of container traffic. 5814 was unique in carrying the Vos Logistics black and red livery; the other two in the fleet carried ACTS blue and yellow colours.

58039 (5811) and 6703, Rotterdam Waalhaven, 20 June 2008.

58039 (5811) and 1254, Middelburg, 22 June 2008. Mercia Charters 'Blaze of Glory' railtour.

8. France: LGV Rhin-Rhône Class 58s

The French LGV Rhin-Rhône project followed in 2009, with twenty-four (now DB Schenker) Class 58s moving to the **Villersexel** base between June and November 2009 for construction work between Villers-les-Pots (near Dijon) and Les Petit Croix (near Belfort). This included the three otherwise redundant Dutch ACTS Class 58s which were transferred direct to France without returning to the UK. Interestingly, of the twenty-four Class 58s deployed on the LGV Rhin-Rhône project, fourteen had previously operated on the LGV Est line.

The Class 58s were painted in all-over yellow livery, with twelve carrying ETF (Eurovia Travaux Ferroviaires) decals (and green waist-line stripe) and twelve carrying TSO (Travaux du Sud Ouest) embellishments; this suggested a degree of sectorisation although in reality they operated as a 'common-user' fleet.

Tracklaying work commenced in June 2009. Sleepers, rails and ballast were brought in by rail through a connection between Lure and the Villersexel base, at which point the Class 58s and other motive power moved the material to site via a temporary connection to the 'trace'. Like the LGV Est, electrification masts were erected prior to tracklaying and involved road transportation. On completion of work in late-2010, the twenty-four Class 58s were booked to move to the ECR site at Alizay for safe storage pending further LGV contract work; in the event, twenty-three arrived at Alizay, with one only making it as far as Woippy Yard near Metz, due to wheelset issues.

A surprising and not widely known feature of the LGV Rhin-Rhône project was the deployment of five ECR Class 66s during the closing months upto September 2010. The Class 66s operated singly on ballast trains and led to the early retirement of a number of Class 58s. The Class 66s involved were 66123/91, 66239/43/9. On completion of work on the Rhin-Rhône, the Class 66s moved back to the UK for use on the Autumn RHTT services.

Summary:

Loco No.	Prepared at	Ex-UK	Liveries
58001	**Eastleigh**	**13/08/09**	**ETF ETFlogo (lhc/rhc/f) Black solebar**
58004	**Eastleigh**	**24/07/09**	**TSO TSOlogo (lhc/rhc/f)**
	Noted en route: Montmédy vers Longuyon, 28/07/09.		
58005	**Eastleigh**	**20/06/09**	**ETF (no green stripe) ETFlogo (lhc/rhc/f) Black solbar**
58006	**Eastleigh**	**24/11/09**	**ETF ETFlogo (lhc/rhc/f) Black solebar, no green stripe.**

Loco No.	Prepared at	Ex-UK	Liveries
58007	Eastleigh	04/06/09	TSO TSOlogo (lhc/rhc/f)
58009	Eastleigh	11/05/09	TSO TSOlogo (lhc/rhc/f)
Noted: Lure yard, 21/05/09.			
58010	Eastleigh	02/07/09	TSO TSOlogo (lhc/rhc/f)
58011	Eastleigh	04/06/09	TSO TSOlogo (lhc/rhc/f)
58013	Eastleigh	24/07/09	ETF ETFlogo (lhc/rhc/f) Black solebar
Noted en route: Montmédy vers Longuyon, 28/07/09.			
58018	Eastleigh	11/06/09	TSO TSOlogo (lhc/rhc/f)
Noted en route: Culmont Chalindrey, 17/06/09.			
58021	Eastleigh	23/10/09	ETF ETFlogo (lhc/rhc/f) Black solebar
58026	Eastleigh	20/06/09	TSO TSOlogo (lhc/rhc/f)
58032	Eastleigh	02/07/09	ETF ETFlogo (lhc/rhc/f) Black solebar
58033	Eastleigh	11/05/09	TSO TSOlogo (lhc/rhc/f)
Noted: Lure yard, 21/05/09.			
58034	Eastleigh	11/05/09	TSO TSOlogo (lhc/rhc/f)
Noted: Lure yard, 21/05/09.			
58035	Eastleigh	20/06/09	TSO TSOlogo (lhc/rhc/f)
58036	Eastleigh	11/09/09	ETF ETFlogo (lhc/rhc/f) Black solebar
58038	Rotterdam	28/07/09 ex NL	ETF ETFlogo (lhc/rhc/f) Blue solebar
Transferred direct from ACTS operations in Holland. Ex-ACTS 5814.			
58039	Rotterdam	28/07/09 ex NL	ETF ETFlogo (lhc/rhc/f) Blue solebar
Transferred direct from ACTS operations in Holland. Ex-ACTS 5811.			
58040	Eastleigh	16/07/09	TSO TSOlogo (lhc/rhc/f)
58042	Eastleigh	20/08/09	ETF ETFlogo (lhc/rhc/f) Black solebar

Loco No.	Prepared at	Ex-UK	Liveries
58044	**Rotterdam**	**28/07/09 ex NL**	**ETF ETFlogo (lhc/rhc/f) Blue solebar**

Transferred direct from ACTS operations in Holland. Ex-ACTS 5812.

58046	**Eastleigh**	**02/07/09**	**TSO TSOlogo (lhc/rhc/f)**
58049	**Eastleigh**	**16/07/09**	**ETF ETFlogo (lhc/rhc/f) Black solebar**

Abbreviations:

Logo positions: lhc: left-hand cabside, rhc: right-hand cabside, f: cab front.

Additional Notes:

58004/7/9-11/8/21/32-5/40/6/9 previously operated on the LGV Est project, plus 58038/9/44 in Holland. It was the first time abroad for 58001/5/6/13/26/36/42.

All locomotive numbers were modified from 580xx to 58-0xx.

TSO locomotives carried blue solebars and ETF locomotives generally had black solebars. However, 58038/9/44 had their solebars painted blue (either an error or the original intention may have been for these locomotives to be TSO-liveried machines).

Locomotives were booked for transfer to Alizay for storage following completion of work. Observations en route to Alizay and arrival dates are as follows:

58001 Lure: 28/09/10, Somain: 30/01/11+21/02/11, Grande-Synthe, Dunkerque: 09/03/11, Calais Fréthun: 12/03/11. Arrived Alizay: 16/03/11.

58004 Culmont-Chalindrey: 30/08/10, Calais Fréthun: 04/10/10+09/10/10. Arrived Alizay by 23/10/10.

58005 Lure: 07/05/11. Arrived Alizay: 13/06/11.

58006 Calais Fréthun: 04/10/10+09/10/10. Arrived Alizay by 23/10/10.

58007 Arrived Alizay: 22/06/11.

58009 Lure: 07/05/11, Hazebrouck: 30/06/11, Calais Fréthun: 01/07/11. Arrived Alizay: 25/07/11.

58010 Lure: 07/05/11. Arrived Alizay: 13/06/11.

58011 Culmont-Chalindrey: 30/08/10, Calais Fréthun: 04/10/10+09/10/10. Arrived Alizay by 23/10/10.

58013 Somain: 30/01/11+210211, Grande-Synthe, Dunkerque: 09/03/11, Calais Fréthun: 12/03/11. Arrived Alizay: 16/03/11.

58018 Lure: 07/05/11, Hazebrouck: 30/06/11, Calais Fréthun: 01/07/11. Arrived Alizay: 25/07/11.

58021 Lure: 07/05/11, Hazebrouck: 30/06/11, Calais Fréthun: 01/07/11. Arrived Alizay: 25/07/11.

58026 Culmont-Chalindrey: 30/08/10, Calais Fréthun: 04/10/10+091010. Arrived Alizay by 23/10/10.

58032 Lure: 07/05/11. Arrived Alizay: 13/06/11.

58033 Arrived Alizay: 22/06/11.

58034 Somain: 30/01/11+21/02/11, Grande-Synthe, Dunkerque: 09/03/11, Calais Fréthun: 12/03/11. Arrived Alizay: 16/03/11.

58035 Arrived Alizay: 22/06/11.

58036	Arrived Alizay: 22/06/11.
58038	Lure: 28/09/10, Somain: 30/01/11+21/02/11, Grande-Synthe, Dunkerque: 09/03/11, Calais Fréthun: 12/03/11. Arrived Alizay: 16/03/11.
58039	Lure: 07/05/11. Arrived Alizay: 13/06/11.
58040	Culmont-Chalindrey: 30/08/10, Calais Fréthun: 04/10/10+09/10/10. Arrived Alizay by 23/10/10.
58042	Somain: 30/01/11+21/02/11, Grande-Synthe, Dunkerque: 09/03/11, Calais Fréthun: 12/03/11. Arrived Alizay: 16/03/11.
58044	Culmont-Chalindrey: 30/08/10. Removed from train with wheelset issues at Woippy, Metz and stored in Yard.
58046	Hazebrouck: 30/06/11, Calais Fréthun: 01/07/11. Arrived Alizay: 25/07/11.
58049	Culmont-Chalindrey: 30/08/10, Calais Fréthun: 04/10/10+09/10/10. Arrived Alizay by 23/10/10.

Summary of Alizay arrival dates:
By 23/10/10: 58004/6/11/26/40/9, 16/03/11: 58001/13/34/8/42, 13/06/11: 58005/10/32/9, 22/06/11: 58007/33/5/6, 25/07/11: 58009/18/21/46.

Disposition of locomotives at Alizay:
05/09/11

SE   NW

    58006/049/004/011/040/026/013/034/042/038/001

       58039/032/005/010/033/035/007/036/018/009/021/046

14/07/13

SE   NW

    58006/049/004/011/040/026/013/034/042/038/001/032/005/010

        58033/035/007/036/018/009/021/046/039

58013 and 58001, Villersexel, 8 July 2010. The Château de Villersexel forms an impressive back-drop to the LGV engineering base.

58001+58013, 58026+58046, 58009+58040, 58034+58021, Villersexel, 8 July 2010. An evening line-up of motive power having returned to base after a day's work on the trace.

58026 alongside 58038, Villersexel, 8 July 2010. Comparative liveries (ETF and TSO) and front ends, with 58038 illustrating the modified light cluster arrangement required when operating for ACTS in the Netherlands. Technically, 58038 should have received a black solebar.

58006 and 58011, Villersexel, 8 July 2010. It is believed that 58006 never worked whilst in France, being used as a source of spares.

58013, Villersexel, 14 September 2009. Derailed and causing mayhem for trains trying to return to Villersexel from the 'trace'.

58011, with 58038 and 58046, Villersexel (D9 bridge looking north), 14 September 2009. 58011 on the rear of a rake of empty ballast hoppers returning to Villersexel on the long spur between the LGV trace and the base itself. Today the railway line has been completely removed and a new northern road route (D486) has been constructed on the old track-bed to by-pass Villersexel village.

58009 and 58034, Villersexel (D9 bridge looking south-east), 14 September 2009. 58009 and 58034 topping and tailing a rake of empty temporary track panel wagons.

58005 and 58035, Villersexel (D9 bridge looking south), 5 July 2010. The spur between the Villersexel base and the LGV trace was the only stretch of track where photography was possible without overhead line equipment, and, for that reason, was a very popular location for seeing the early morning and evening processions.

58034 and 58021, plus 58005, La Pâture, 6 July 2010. The temporary trackbed here has now returned to farmland and if you visited this location today you would be very hard pressed to believe that any railway infrastructure ever existed.

58007, plus 2xMak1206, La Pâture, 6 July 2010. The bridge carries the D9 road and the immediate surrounding area is now the D9/D486 junction.

58026 and 58046, Le Grand Magny, 8 July 2010. This was the location where the spur from Villersexel base joined the LGV route, hence the clutter of the overhead line equipment. An early morning ballast departure heading east straight into the rising sun.

58035 and 58049, plus 58039, Marloz, 14 September 2009.

58026 and 58018, plus 58005 alongside 58046 and 58038, plus 58011, Anthon, 15 September 2009. Two ballast trains awaiting discharging.

58004 and 58042, Aibres, 5 July 2010. 58004 desperately trying to imitate a Class 56!

58032 and 58036, plus 58042 and 58004, Laire, 5 July 2010. 58032 giving 58004 some stiff competion on the 'clag' front!

58009 and 58040, with 58044 and 58033, Bois de Châtenois, 7 July 2010. Note that the locomotives are operating on temporary timber sleepered track panels without ballast, the first stage of the tracklaying process. The welded rails will be discharged from the train (seen here) on either side of the temporary track, awaiting the replacement of the track panels with initial shallow ballasting and concrete sleepers.

58018 and 58039, Chavanne, 8 July 2010. Entering the tunnel at slow speed prior to dropping ballast. Note the dust-extraction equipment at the tunnel entrance.

58006, Alizay, 5 September 2011. 58006 stored at Alizay (near Rouen); this locomotive never received the ETF green bodyside stripe.

58046, Alizay, 5 September 2011. 58046 at Alizay, along with 22 other examples, following the completion of work on the LGV Rhin-Rhône. At the time of writing (July 2019) these twenty-three locomotives still lie dormant at Alizay. Substantial deterioration following eight years of inactivity, combined with visitations from French 'copper-fairies', mean that scrapping is their most likely future.

58044, Woippy, 26 June 2014. 58044 never made it to Alizay, succumbing to wheelset problems near Metz.

9. Spain: Class 58s

The first two Class 58s moved to Spain via the Channel Tunnel in April 2003 and were delivered as replacements for accident-damaged Class 37s. A further six followed in 2004, with the final four arriving in 2008.

The working arrangements for the Class 58s were very similar to those which applied for the Spanish Class 37s covered earlier i.e.

- hired by Continental Rail (CR) (a sub-contractor to GIF, subsequently ADIF),
- relatively short periods of intense activity combined with long periods of inactivity between progressive contracts,
- new continuously-welded rail movements from the main base to site, and, 'final' ballast movements from numerous remote 'virtual quarries' to discharge points,
- low-loader road transfers to 'leap-frog' from one operating base to the next (reflecting the construction methods deployed, the non-contiguous nature of many of the contracts operated by the Class 58s along the routes, and, the Iberian 1668mm gauge on 'classic' Spanish routes).

The lines where the Class 58s were deployed are as follows:-

Calatyud/Lleida (Madrid-Barcelona)
The first Spanish arrivals, 58041/3, were noted at Irun Kostorbe on 18 April 2003 awaiting road transport for the final part of their journey to **Calatyud** base; 58043 was off-loaded from a low-loader at Miraflores (near Zaragoza) on 7 May 2003. Both 58041 and 58043 were noted at Calatyud on 28 August 2003. 58041 was subsequently seen at **Montagut/Raimat** base on 22 October 2003

and 23 February 2004, and 58043 at **Puigverd de Lleida** base on 17 June 2004 and 29 October 2004. These two locomotives presumably undertook tracklaying work from the respective bases but no photographic evidence has been seen to substantiate this.

Córdoba-Málaga (Madrid-Málaga)
Six EWS Class 58s (58020/4/5/9-31) were shipped from Newport Docks on 23 May 2004, utilising the Jumbo Shipping vessel *Fairload*, arriving at Sevilla 27 May 2004. They were moved by road transport to gain access to the 'standard gauge' high-speed line near Sevilla and then by rail to the AVE base at **Almodóvar del Rio** (15km south of Córdoba). In addition, 58041 and 58043 were transferred under their own power from the Lleida area to Almodóva del Rio via the high-speed lines during May and November 2004 respectively, initially overnight to Madrid, followed by a second overnight movement to Almodóva. This made a fleet total of eight locomotives for the construction of the Córdoba-Málaga extension. Headlight and air-conditioning modifications were undertaken at Almodóvar, together with the reinstatement of Qtron equipment, internal cab painting and other repair work (brake tests, low-power checks, etc).

58041 was subsequently noted at Mesas de Guadalora base being loaded up for road transfer to Bobadilla on 21 July 2004; Mesas was a major base on the Cordoba to Sevilla AVE line. 58024/5/30/43 were subsequently moved by road from Almodóva to the base at **Bobadilla** in November 2004, leaving 58020/9/31 to work from Almodóvar.

Work on the Córdoba-Málaga extension started in November 2004 with the Class 58s operating from the two bases (plus associated remote ballast dumps) and by mid-2006 the route was largely complete between the Almodóvar del Rio junction (where the line to

Málaga diverged from the Madrid-Sevilla AVE line) and the Abdalajís tunnel south of Bobadilla. The joining of the initially separate work undertaken from Almodóva and Bobadilla enabled the two fleets of Class 58s to become a combined fleet of eight for a while. The 96.8km line from Almodóvar del Rio-Antequera Santa Ana station (actually at Bobadilla) was inaugurated on 16 December 2006.

In July 2006, four Class 58s (58020/4/5/30) were moved by road from Bobadilla to Los Prados, west of Málaga, to commence tracklaying work northwards to the Abdalajís tunnel. By mid-July 2007, the Antequera-Málaga section of the line was declared by ADIF to be over 90% complete, the remaining elements being the geologically challenging Abdalajís tunnel and the Málaga terminal. Once the Abdalajís gap had been completed, it became possible once again for the two sub-fleets to mingle, and 58041 from Bobadilla, at least, was seen in Málaga in December 2007. The 57.7km Antequera Santa Ana-Málaga section was inaugurated on 23 December 2007. On completion of work the full remaining fleet of seven Class 58s (see below) congregated at Bobadilla.

Olmedo-Valladolid (Madrid-Valladolid)
With the four Class 58s at Bobadilla being essentially surplus to requirements by end-2006, 58031 was moved from Bobadilla to north-west Spain during 2007 to work on the Madrid-Valladolid AVE line based at **Olmedo**, being noted working at Valladolid on 15 September 2007 and 1 October 2007. The Madrid-Segovia-Valladolid line (179.6km) was inaugurated on 22 December 2007.

Albacete/València
The Levante high-speed line effectively commenced at a diverging junction off the Madrid-Sevilla line at Torrejón de Velasco (28km from Madrid Atocha), heading east to Cuenca, then swinging south and dividing at Motilla del Palancar, with one arm continuing south to Albacete (and including subsequent extensions to Alicante and Murcia), and the other heading eastwards, via Utiel and Requena, to València.

Tracklaying began in 2008, initially from Albacete northwards. The eight locomotives already in Spain (58020/4/5/9-31/41/3) were moved to **Albacete** base between July and December 2008 (58020/5 being noted loaded onto road transport at Bobadilla on 7 July 2008)

for use on the tracklaying trains from Albacete to Motilla del Palanca junction (70km) and onto **Gabaldón** base (a further 4km). By mid-November 2008, ADIF announced that the 74km between Albacete and Gabaldón were complete, following five months of work. Having reached Gabaldón, tracklaying by the Class 58s continued north to an unknown point believed to be just south of Cuenca, and also eastwards towards Requena, albeit with the continuously welded rails still being supplied from Albacete via the new trace.

Four additional Class 58 locomotives (58015/27/47/50) moved via the Channel Tunnel in September 2008 to work from the **Requena-Utiel** base for work eastwards to València (65km) and westwards to Motilla del Palancar (80km). Initially these four locomotives worked in isolation but once the link was made at a point adjacent to the Contreras reservoirs in about July/August 2009 the combined Levante Class 58 fleet became twelve-strong.

During 2010, the Class 58 saw increasingly limited use and were progressively stored at Albacete pending developments, with 58041 and 58043 finding occasional use in the Albacete area until at least March 2011. The Madrid-Cuenca-Motilla-València line (399.8km) was inaugurated on 15 December 2010, followed by Motilla-Albacete on 18 December 2010.

Extension to Alicante/Murcia
The next contract was the extension from Albacete to Alicante (171.5km) via Almansa, and in December 2010 Class 58s started to move from Albacete to the **Monforte del Cid** base, again by road transport, to undertake tracklaying work eastwards to Alicante (circa 22km) and northwards to Villena (and possibly as far as La Encina). 58031 and 58047 were the first to leave Albacete on 16 December 2010, and by 3 March 2011 58015/20/4/9-31/47 were in Montforte del Cid. Work started from Montforte during April 2011, using six out of the seven locomotives.

On 12 July 2011, 58015/20/4/9-31/47, the seven at Monforte del Cid, were deleted from the UK TOPS system, with ownership transferring to Transfesa (a subsidiary of DB); 58041/3, both still stored at Albacete at this point, were similarly removed from TOPS on 12 September 2011. The remaining three, 58025/7/50, remained under DB ownership stored out of use at Albacete. 58043 migrated from Albacete to Monforte del Cid sometime between May 2012 and December 2013, whilst 58041, with engine problems, remained stored at Albacete.

By May 2012, the seven Class 58s were deployed laying ballast on the urban outskirts of Alicante, but by the end of the year they must have become surplus to requirements yet again given that the Albacete-Alicante line was inaugurated on 18 June 2013.

Storage at Monforte del Cid followed through 2013-15 until further rejuvenation for work on the Monforte del Cid-Murcia section (67.7km) followed in 2015/16. By February 2016, two of the Class 58s from Monforte del Cid (58020/31) had found their way to Los Ramos/Alquerias, near Murcia, again via low-loader to bridge the Orihuela gap. Two Class 58s, 58029/47, saw little (if any) deployment on the Murcia line due to engine problems.

In May 2016, 58024 was noted on ballast duties from the La Encina triangle, working on the branch towards Xativa. Judging by the distances travelled to get to the ballasting locations, this locomotive may have been out-stationed at La Encina for some time.

With the Class 58s having now been resident in Spain for between ten and fifteen years, it is inevitable that some have fallen by the wayside. At the beginning of 2017, the 'DB Three' were out of traffic (and had been for six years), and three of the Transfesa locomotives (58029/41/7) were stored with engine defects, leaving only six locomotives available for 'immediate' use (58015/20/4/30/1/43).

Liveries

The first eight Class 58s were delivered to Spain in GIF light blue livery with broad dark blue bodyside band, as per the Class 37s. When GIF became ADIF on 1 January 2005, most if not all locomotives lost their bodyside GIF lettering. The final four locomotives (58015/27/47/50) were delivered in the darker blue Continental Rail livery with a yellow waist band. From late-2008/early-2009, the GIF-liveried Class 58s followed suit and were repainted into the Continental Rail livery. Continental Rail L-series numbers were applied to most locomotives (see table), although 58015 is believed to have never carried an L-number whilst in Spain, and 58025 is believed never to have carried an L-number since its repaint into Continental Rail colours.

Summary (as at November 2018):-

Loco. No.	GIF No.	Prepared at	Date Ex-UK	GIF Liveries/logos (with last date seen)	CR Liveries/logos (with first date seen)	Operating Base History (Main Locations)	Current Owner/Location
58015	(L54)	EH	18/09/08	--------	CR nlogo fye (L54 not carried)	Requena/Albacete/ Monforte del Cid	Transfesa/Monforte del Cid

Believed that the allocated L54 number has never been carried, possibly given the confusion initially surrounding 58027 (see below).

| 58020 | L43 | OC/EH | 23/05/04 | GIF GIFlogo ½ye LBWS&CWB (24/07/08) | CR nlogo fye (29/03/09) | Bobadilla/Malaga/ Albacete/ Monforte del Cid | Transfesa/Monforte del Cid |

Lifted onto low-loader at Bobadilla 07/07/08, ready for movement to Albacete.

| 58024 | L42 | OC/EH/CF | 23/05/04 | GIF GIFlogo ½ye LBWS&CWB (24/07/08) | CR nlogo fye (29/03/09) | Almodóvar del Rio/ Bobadilla/ Malaga/Albacete/ Monforte del Cid | Transfesa/Monforte del Cid |

Lifted onto low-loader at Almodóvar del Rio 15/11/04; off-loaded at Bobadilla 16/11/04.
Off-loaded from low-loader at Monforte del Cid 22/12/10 (ex Albacete).

Loco. No.	GIF No.	Prepared at	Date Ex-UK	GIF Liveries/logos (with last date seen)	CR Liveries/logos (with first date seen)	Operating Base History (Main Locations)	Current Owner/Location
58025	L41	EH/CF	23/05/04	GIF GIFlogo fye Black CWB (28/04/09)	CR nlogo fye (L41 not carried) (08/08/09)	Almodóvar del Rio/ Bobadilla/Albacete	DB/Albacete (stored)

Lifted onto low-loader at Almodóvar del Rio 18/11/04; off-loaded at Bobadilla 18/11/04.
Lifted onto low-loader at Bobadilla 07/07/08, ready for movement to Albacete.

Loco. No.	GIF No.	Prepared at	Date Ex-UK	GIF Liveries/logos (with last date seen)	CR Liveries/logos (with first date seen)	Operating Base History (Main Locations)	Current Owner/Location
58027	L52	EH	18/09/08	———	CR nlogo fye	Requena/Albacete	DB/Albacete (stored)

Off-loaded from low-loader at Requena 29/09/08.
Originally numbered L54 on arrival in Spain, but subsequently renumbered L52 during December 2008.

Loco. No.	GIF No.	Prepared at	Date Ex-UK	GIF Liveries/logos (with last date seen)	CR Liveries/logos (with first date seen)	Operating Base History (Main Locations)	Current Owner/Location
58029	L44	EH/CF	23/05/04	GIF GIFlogo fye Yellow[1]/Black[2] CWB (02/10/09)	CR nlogo fye (01/01/10)	Bobadilla/Albacete/ Monforte del Cid	Transfesa/Monforte del Cid (stored)
58030	L46	EH/CF	23/05/04	GIF GIFlogo fye Black CWB (28/04/09)	CR nlogo fye (01/01/10)	Almodóvar del Rio/ Bobadilla/ Malaga/Albacete/ Monforte del Cid	Transfesa/Monforte del Cid

Lifted onto low-loader at Almodóvar del Rio 16/11/04; off-loaded at Bobadilla 17/11/04.
Lifted onto low-loader at Bobadilla 23/07/08, ready for movement to Albacete.

Loco. No.	GIF No.	Prepared at	Date Ex-UK	GIF Liveries/logos (with last date seen)	CR Liveries/logos (with first date seen)	Operating Base History (Main Locations)	Current Owner/Location
58031	L45	EH	23/05/04	GIF GIFlogo fye Yellow CWB (01/10/07)	CR nlogo fye (26/06/09)	Bobadilla/Valladolid/ Albacete/ Monforte del Cid	Transfesa/Monforte del Cid

Lifted for bogie change 26/06/09.
Noted awaiting loading onto low-loader at Albacete 16/12/10; noted awaiting off-loading at Monforte del Cid 20/12/10.

Loco. No.	GIF No.	Prepared at	Date Ex-UK	GIF Liveries/logos (with last date seen)	CR Liveries/logos (with first date seen)	Operating Base History (Main Locations)	Current Owner/Location
58041	L36	EH	05/04/03	GIF GIFlogo fye Yellow CWB (11/02/09)	CR nlogo fye (29/03/09)	Calatyud/Puigverd de Lleida/Bobadilla/ Malaga/Albacete	Transfesa/Albacete (stored)

Noted at Irun Plaiaundi 15/04/03 and Irun Kostorbe 18/04/03.
Lifted onto low-loader at Irun Kostorbe 23/04/03.
Moved from Puigverd de Lleida to Calatyud 15/05/04, from Calatyud to Madrid 16/05/04, from Madrid to Mora 28/05/04 and from Mora to Almodovar 29/05/04 (all night time movements via the new AVE line).
Loaded onto low-loader at Mesas de Guadalora 21/07/04, prior to movement to Bobadilla
Carries EVN 93.71.13.52.541-7.

Loco. No.	GIF No.	Prepared at	Date Ex-UK	GIF Liveries/logos (with last date seen)	CR Liveries/logos (with first date seen)	Operating Base History (<u>Main</u> Locations)	Current Owner/ Location
58043	L37	EH	05/04/03	GIF GIFlogo fye Yellow CWB (11/02/09)	CR nlogo fye (29/03/09)	Calatyud/Raimat/Almodóvar del Rio/Bobadilla/Malaga/ Albacete/Monforte del Cid	Transfesa/Monforte Del Cid

Noted at Irun Plaiaundi 15/04/03 and Irun Kostorbe 18/04/03+23/04/03.
Off-loaded from low-loader at Miraflores (east of Zaragoza) 07/05/03.
Moved from Madrid to Almodóvar 06/11/04 (night time movement via the new AVE line).
Lifted onto low-loader at Almodóvar del Rio 12/11/04; off-loaded at Bobadilla 13/11/04.
Carries EVN 93.71.13.52.543-3.

58047	L51	EH/ Northam	18/09/08	-- -- --	CR nlogo fye	Requena/Albacete/ Monforte del Cid	Transfes/Monforte del Cid (stored)

Lifted onto low-loader at Albacete 16/12/10; due to be off-loaded at Monforte del Cid 18/12/10.

58050	L53	EH	18/09/08	-- -- --	CR nlogo fye	Requena/Albacete	DB/Albacete (stored)

Abbreviations:

Prepared at: CF: Cardiff Canton, EH: Eastleigh, OC: Old Oak Common.

GIF Livery details: ½ye: Half yellow cab front ends, fye: Full yellow cab front ends, LBWS: Light blue front window surrounds, CWB: Front cab window beading.

CR Livery details: nlogo: No logo, fye: Full yellow cab front ends.

Additional Notes:-

58015/27/47/50 had previously worked in France (LGV Est).
58041 and 58043 were fitted with the ASFA signalling system to allow them to run on the new AVE line. It is believed that the system was only used once when they travelled light engine from Lleida to Almodóvar via Madrid. This movement also probably explains the allocation of EVN numbers to these two locomotives.
58031 was named *Caballero Ferroviario* during 2007.

58041 (L36) and 37799 (L27), Montagut, 23 February 2004. A fairly rare shot of a Class 58 and a Class 37 together in Spain which, it is believed, only took place at Catalyud, Montagut and Puigverd de Lleida. *(Keith Butler)*

58041 (L36), Mesas de Guadalora, 21 July 2004. Being craned onto a low-loader prior to movement to Bobadilla. *(Keith Butler)*

58043 (L37) and 58031 (L45), Bobadilla, 5 July 2006.

58020 (L43), 58030 (L46), 58025 (L41), Bobadilla Viaduct 6 July 2006. 58020, 58030 and 58025 are seen undertaking viaduct stress testing duties near Bobadilla. 58041 (L36), undertaking the same duties, is just visible above the wagon to the right of the picture. Note the different front-end liveries of 58020 and 58030.

58020 (L43), 58030 (L46), 58025 (L41), 58041 (L36), Bobadilla Viaduct, 6 July 2006. Ancient and modern!

58030 (L46) and 58029 (L44), Rubielos Bajos, 27 April 2009. Long welded rails being delivered from Albacete to the trace north of Gabaldón.

58029 (L44) and 58030 (L46), Gabaldón 27 April 2009. 58020 can be seen in the distance at the junction with the Gabaldón ADIF base.

58029 (L44) and 58020, Gabaldón, 27 April 2009. 58029 (L44) and 58020 are seen completing ballast discharging duties on the AVE trace north of Gabaldón. Note the mixed liveries, with 58029 carrying the original GIF livery (albeit now without the GIF lettering) and 58020 recently repainted into the darker blue Continental Rail blue livery with yellow stripe. At this time, 58020 was not carrying its allocated L43 number.

58043 and 58024, Castellejo, 27 April 2009. 58043 immediately following repainting into Continental Rail livery at the Castellejo remote ballast dump with no numbers at all.

58030 (L46), between Gabaldón and Almodovar del Pinar, 28 April 2009. 58030 manoeuvring a rail train in preparation for discharging.

58027 (L52), Requena Utiel, 28 April 2009. 58027 with a rake of ballast wagons in the process of being loaded. The Class 58 had been in Spain for less than six months, hence its near pristine condition.

58047 (L51) side-by-side with 58050 (L53), Chiva 'virtual quarry', 29 April 2009. A very Spanish landscape; shame about the catenary poles!

58031 (L45), Gabaldón, 26 June 2009. Bogie-change at Gabaldón. *(Jose-Ramon Corbacho)*

58043 (L37) and 58047 (L51), Gabaldón, 15 December 2009. Snow in Spain! *(Jose-Ramon Corbacho)*

58047 (L51) and 58027 (L52), Gabaldón, 15 December 2009. Tunnel-cleaning train. *(Jose-Ramon Corbacho)*

58050 (L53), 58027 (L52) and 58025, Albacete, 6 May 2012. All three locomotives stored out of use.

58015 and 58030 (L46), Alicante, 8 May 2012. Ballast train shuttle duties on the outskirts of Alicante.

58015 and 58030 (L46), Alicante, 8 May 2012. Shuttling empty wagons back to the remote ballast dump.

58015 and 58024 (L42), Alicante, 9 May 2012. 58015 now with 58024 performing similar duties a day later, in this instance leading the train of empty wagons from Monforte de Cid Base to the ballast dump for loading.

58015 and 58024 (L42), Alicante, 9 May 2012. Loading underway, and after running round the train, the Class 58s propelled the train on towards 'down-town' Alicante for discharge.

58029 (L44), 58047 (L51) and 58043 (L37), Monforte del Cid, 9 May 2016. A RENFE high speed train from Alicante to Madrid passes Monforte del Cid base. 58029, 58047 and 58043 are stabled in the yard. The 'extension' from Monforte del Cid to Murcia can be seen in the left middle distance.

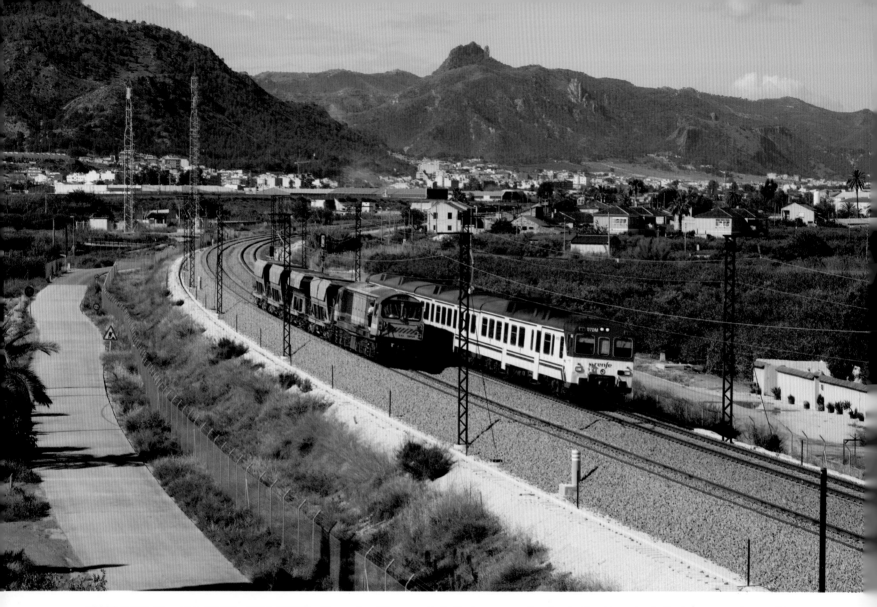

58020 (L43), Alquerias, 11 May 2016. 58020 with a rake of four empty ballast wagons returning to the Alquerias ballast dump on the outskirts of Murcia, passing a RENFE diesel multiple unit. The left hand track is standard-gauge (part of the Monforte del Cid to Murcia AVE line), and the right hand track is Iberian-gauge.

58020 (L43), Alquerias, 11 May 2016. Departing from Alquerias with ballast wagons to be discharged on the western approaches of the Callosa tunnel.

58024 (L42), La Encina, 12 May 2016. 58024 on the La Encina triangle ballast loading pad awaiting its next turn of duty. This work is associated with another 'extension' from the Madrid-Alicant line from La Encina towards Xativa.

10. Bulgaria: BZK Class 87s

From the mid-2000s, private concerns became increasingly involved in the facilitation of British motive power operating abroad, notably trading companies, leasing companies (ROSCOs [Rolling Stock Companies] such as Porterbrook and HSBC) and management companies such as Europhoenix and their engineering arm Electric Traction Services.

In late-2006, Porterbrook sold 87012/9 to БЖК (BZK), or ВБЛГАРСКА ЖЕЛЕЗОПЪТНА КОМПАНИЯ (literally translated Bulgarian Railway Company), via trading company Romic-Ace International; these two locomotives moved from Wembley to Bulgaria via the Channel Tunnel for trial purposes in December 2006, still retaining their Network South-East and LNW black liveries respectively. Transit across Europe was very slow with the two locomotives still in Calais in mid-February 2007; one month later and they were transitting Austria. On arrival, the two locomotives were modified at Koncar, Sofia, in readiness for testing; by end-June 2007 initial modifications had been completed which involved the fitting of twin air-pipes, wing mirrors, relocation of the front-end box spotlights from a position just above the buffer beam to just below the cab windows (to give a delta-lighting pattern) and revamped cab instrumentation. БЖК signage and running number check-digits were also applied at this time. Extensive trials were undertaken and it was not until July/August 2008 that 87012/9 received the additional modifications which ultimately became the norm for all new arrivals i.e. snow ploughs, roof-mounted 'Shrek' air horns, roof-mounted lights (replacing the box lights) and bodyside transformer access panels. Pictures exist of the fully modified 'finished articles' (87012/9) alongside the newly arrived 87007/8/26 at Koncar on 24 July 2008.

Trials with 87012/9 had clearly been successful and the intention was to ship a further twenty-five Class 87s to Bulgaria. In the event, only fifteen locomotives were transferred between June 2008 and November 2009, making seventeen in total, this being due to the adverse impact of the 2008 economic recession. Of the additional fifteen, three were moved via the Channel Tunnel, and the remainder conventionally shipped via Hull, with, it is believed, barge transfer from Antwerp to Ruse.

Considerable preparation work on the fifteen was undertaken by ETS (Electric Traction Services) at Long Marston, including the repainting of 87004 into BR blue livery and nine others in the green and yellow BZK livery. 87006/22/28 were transferred in their touched-up DRS/First dark-blue livery, and 87007/08 in Cotswold grey. Final 'Bulgarianisation' was carried out at Koncar, Sofia, including all of the modifications listed above. The BZK fleet have, so far, never been provided with a second pantograph.

87004/12/19/22 are the only locomotives to have been repainted since arrival in Bulgaria, all in subtle variations of their as-exported liveries, 87004/12/9 as planned repaints and 87022 following extensive fire damage. Unfortunately during the July 2018 repaint, 87004 lost its cab side numbers and BR double-arrow emblem leaving only BZK markings, red nameplates, and full EVN numbers positioned centrally on the bodysides.

87014 has never worked in Bulgaria, and resided at Koncar, Sofia, following arrival in late 2009 until it was transferred to

CERB, Sofia during 2017, and on to Express Service, Ruse in March 2019. 87008 has also been stored out of use since 2011 following copper theft and is now used as a source of spares, sitting on a pair of accommodation bogies.

The BZK Class 87s are based at Pirdop and over the past ten years have operated extensively throughout Bulgaria. However, there have been three main traffic flows which have formed the backbone of their activity in Bulgaria:-

Sulphuric acid (a by-product of copper-refining) from Pirdop to Razdelna (near Varna),

Copper-ore from the Black Sea port of Burgas to the Pirdop refinery, and,

A daily freight service from Razdelna to Ruse Razpredelitelna (carrying general merchandise and stone products from the quarries at Senovo and Vetovo).

In addition, the BZK Class 87s found useful employment on various contracted and spot-hire flows which took them to various destinations including Ilyantsi, Blagoevgrad, Plovdiv, etc.

The Class 87s, along with imported Romanian-built Co-Co Class 40 locomotives, were involved with the sulphuric acid trains from the time of their arrival in Bulgaria right up to October 2018 when BZK lost the contract to BDZ Cargo, the national rail operator. BZK deployed the Class 87s on the copper-ore trains from Burgas to Pirdop from December 2016 when they ousted the previous incumbents on this contract (Deutsche Bahn); however, BZK subsequently lost the copper-ore traffic to BDZ at the same time as the sulphuric flow. Both of these flows are now operated

by BDZ Cargo Romanian-built Class 46 locomotives (essentially the same type of locomotive as the BZK Class 40s). The daily Razdelna-Ruse service, however, currently remains in the hands of BZK motive power.

The sulphuric acid trains, in particular, were very impressive with two locomotives on the front of a 42-wagon consist, with a further 'pusher' locomotive on the rear. Unfortunately, for British enthusiasts, the lead locomotive of the front pair was frequently a BZK Class 40 electric; it is understood that the reason for this was the superior adhesion characteristics of these Co-Co locomotives. The second locomotive of the leading pair and the 'pusher' locomotive were usually Class 87s.

Since October 2018, with the loss of the sulphuric acid and copper-ore traffic, the workload for the Class 87s has been drastically reduced inevitably leading to significant numbers of locomotives being seen parked-up. BZK cost-saving initiatives will in all probability mean that Class 87s awaiting transformer and other repairs will not return to service (e.g. 87006/8/10/3/22, plus 87014, seen at Express Service, Ruse on 19 July 2019). Similarly, with BZK now owned by Grup Ferovia Roman (a Romanian-based company), there could well be an on-going preference for the Co-Co Class 40 locomotives over the lower-powered non-indigenous Bo-Bo Class 87s.

The decision in 2008/09 to restrict the Class 87 fleet to seventeen, resulted in eleven 'spare' locomotives in the UK. Recessionary pressures suggested unforeseeable outlets for this number of locomotives, so seven were scrapped at EMR Kingsbury. For the remaining four, Bulgaria once again beckoned (see Section 11).

Summary:-

Orig BZK No. Subseq. EVN	Ex-UK	Prepared At	Certification Date	Works Dates	Liveries	Additional notes
87003-0 91 52 00 **87003**-7	22/12/08 ex-Hull	**ETS Long Marston/ Koncar, Sofia**	03/08/09	**БК: xx/07/09 БК: 02/11/11 ЕС: 07/11/14 ЕС: 08/11/17**	**BZK NOL**	

Orig BZK No. Subseq. EVN	Ex-UK	Prepared At	Certification Date	Works Dates	Liveries	Additional notes
87004-8 91 52 00 <u>87004</u>-5	09/11/09 ex-Hull	ETS Long Marston/ Koncar, Sofia	22/03/10	БК: 21/03/10 БК: 17/07/13 БК: 16/11/16 ЕС: 05/07/18	BFY OL RNp ('*Britannia*')	ETH retained. **Repainted during 05/07/18 works visit.**

Noted Express Service, Obraztsov Chiflik: 06/06/18 (paintwork stripped ready for repainting).

Orig BZK No. Subseq. EVN	Ex-UK	Prepared At	Certification Date	Works Dates	Liveries	Additional notes
87006-3 91 52 00 <u>87006</u>-0	22/12/08 ex-Hull	ETS Long Marston/ Koncar, Sofia	18/05/09	БК: 15/05/09 БК: 15/09/11 ЕС: 01/07/14	DRS/First Blue OL	

Noted stored Express Service, Obraztsov Chiflik: 04/05/16, 09/08/16, 19/04/17, 11/07/17, 18/04/18, 06/06/18, 18/10/18, 19/06/19 (transformer problems).

Orig BZK No. Subseq. EVN	Ex-UK	Prepared At	Certification Date	Works Dates	Liveries	Additional notes
87007-1 91 52 00 <u>87007</u>-8	19/06/08 via Channel Tunnel	ETS Long Marston/ Koncar, Sofia	10/11/08	БК: 31/10/08 БК: 26/11/10 БК: 12/03/14 ЕС: 27/02/17 ЕС: 26/02/19	Cotswold Grey OL	

Observations en route Bulgaria: Calais Fréthun (F): 23/06/08, Vienna Zentalverscheibe (A): 05/07/08, Ebenfurth (A): 05/07/08 (transit).
Noted Koncar, Sofia: 24/07/08, 03/10/08 (undergoing modifications).

Orig BZK No. Subseq. EVN	Ex-UK	Prepared At	Certification Date	Works Dates	Liveries	Additional notes
87008-9 -------	19/06/08 via Channel Tunnel	ETS Long Marston/ Koncar, Sofia	07/10/08	БК: 06/10/08 БК: 27/01/11	Cotswold Grey OL	

Observations en route Bulgaria: Calais Fréthun (F): 23/06/08, Vienna Zentalverscheibe (A): 05/07/08, Ebenfurth (A): 05/07/08 (transit).
Noted Koncar, Sofia: 24/07/08 and 03/10/08 (undergoing modifications).
Noted stored Pirdop: 08/10/11 (copper theft), 16/10/11; Express Service, Obraztsov Chiflik: 09/09/14, 02/09/15, 04/05/16, 09/08/16, 19/04/17, 11/07/17, 18/04/18, 06/06/18, 18/10/18, 19/06/19.
Source of spares; on accommodation bogies.

Orig BZK No. Subseq. EVN	Ex-UK	Prepared At	Certification Date	Works Dates	Liveries	Additional notes
87010-5 91 52 00 <u>87010</u>-2	27/10/08 ex-Hull	ETS Long Marston/ Koncar, Sofia	27/02/09	БК: 19/02/09 БК: 03/06/11 ЕС: 11/07/14 ЕС: 18/09/17	BZK NOL	

Noted stored Express Service, Obraztsov Chiflik: 18/10/18, 19/06/19.

Orig BZK No. Subseq. EVN	Ex-UK	Prepared At	Certification Date	Works Dates	Liveries	Additional notes
87012-1 91 52 00 <u>87012</u>-8	27/12/06 via Channel Tunnel	Wembley/ Koncar, Sofia	No date.	БК: 07/07/07 БК: 07/07/09 БК: 20/10/11 Reloc:19/12/14 ЕС: 14/11/17	NSE OL	**Repainted during 19/12/14 works visit.**

Observations en route Bulgaria: Calais Fréthun: 13/02/07, XX (A): 15/03/07.
Incorrectly given wrong EVN (91 52 00 <u>87012</u>-0) during Reloc SA, Craiova, Romania works visit; check digit subsequently corrected.

Orig BZK No. Subseq. EVN	Ex-UK	Prepared At	Certification Date	Works Dates	Liveries	Additional notes
87013-9 91 52 00 **87013**-6	09/11/09 ex-Hull	ETS Long Marston/ Koncar, Sofia	27/07/10	БК: 21/07/10 БК: 03/10/13 ЕС: 04/11/16	BZK NOL	

Noted Koncar, Sofia: 04/05/10 (awaiting modifications).
Noted stored Express Service, Obraztsov Chiflik: 11/07/17, 18/04/18, 06/06/18, 18/10/18, 19/06/19 (transformer problems).

87014-7 -------	09/11/09 ex-Hull	ETS Long Marston	Not certified.	None.	BZK NOL	**Never entered traffic.**

Noted stored Koncar, Sofia: 08/10/11, 19/09/14, 12/08/16 (source of spares). Disappeared by 10/07/17.
Noted stored CERB, Sofia: 24/10/17.
Noted stored Express Service, Obraztsov Chiflik: 19/06/19 (arrived March 2019).

87019-6 91 52 00 **87019**-3	27/12/06 via Channel Tunnel	Wembley/ Koncar, Sofia	No date.	БК: xx/06/07 БК: xx/06/09 БК: 30/07/10 ЕС: 24/10/13 ЕС: 20/11/15 ЕС: 10/01/19	LNW Black OL	**Repainted during 20/11/15 works visit.**

Observations en route Bulgaria: Calais Fréthun: 13/02/07, XX (A): 15/03/07.

87020-4 91 52 00 **87020**-1	25/05/09 ex-Hull	ETS Long Marston/ Koncar, Sofia	13/10/09	БК: 14/10/09 БК: 11/01/12 ЕС: 23/01/15 ЕС: 09/02/18	BZK NOL	

Noted Koncar, Sofia: 10/10/09 (undergoing modifications).

87022-0 91 52 00 **87022**-7	27/10/08 ex-Hull	ETS Long Marston/ Koncar, Sofia	10/04/09	БК: 09/04/09 БК: 04/05/12 ЕС: 10/09/14 ЕС: 03/10/17	DRS/First Blue OL	**Repainted during 10/09/14 works visit.**

Fire damage at Karnobat xx/12/13. Noted Express Service, Obraztsov Chiflik: 09/09/14 (undergoing repairs). Returned to traffic.
Noted stored Express Service, Obraztsov Chiflik: 02/09/15, 04/05/16, 09/08/16 (transformer problems). Returned to traffic.
Noted stored Express Service, Obraztsov Chiflik: 11/07/17 (awaiting repairs), 18/04/18 (undergoing repairs). Returned to traffic.
Noted stored Express Service, Obraztsov Chiflik: 18/10/18, 19/06/19.

87026-1 91 52 00 **87026**-8	19/06/08 via Channel Tunnel	ETS Long Marston/ Koncar, Sofia	12/09/08	БК: 12/09/08 БК: 23/11/10 БК: 26/03/14 ЕС: 16/03/17	BZK NOL	

Observations en route Bulgaria: Calais Fréthun (F): 23/06/08, Vienna Zentalverscheibe (A): 05/07/08, Ebenfurth (A): 05/07/08 (transit). Noted Koncar, Sofia: 24/07/08.

Orig BZK No. Subseq. EVN	Ex-UK	Prepared At	Certification Date	Works Dates	Liveries	Additional notes
87028-7 91 52 00 **87028**-4	27/10/08 ex-Hull	ETS Long Marston/ Koncar, Sofia	27/03/09	БК: 25/03/09 БК: 25/08/11 БК: 16/10/14 ЕС: 27/10/17	DRS/First Blue OL	
87029-5 91 52 00 **87029**-2	25/05/09 ex-Hull	ETS Long Marston/ Koncar, Sofia	31/08/09	БК: 27/08/09 БК: 20/06/12 ЕС: 16/10/15 ЕС: 14/11/18	BZK NOL	ETH retained.
87033-7 91 52 00 **87033**-4	25/05/09 ex-Hull	ETS Long Marston/ Koncar, Sofia	10/12/09	БК: xx/12/09 БК: 11/05/12 ЕС: 06/11/15 ЕС: 09/10/18	BZK NOL	

Noted Koncar, Sofia: 10/10/09 (undergoing modifications).

Orig BZK No. Subseq. EVN	Ex-UK	Prepared At	Certification Date	Works Dates	Liveries	Additional notes
87034-5 91 52 00 **87034**-2	22/12/08 ex-Hull	ETS Long Marston/ Koncar, Sofia	22/06/09	БК: 10/06/09 БК: 16/12/11 БК: 24/01/15 ЕС: 01/02/18	BZK NOL	Partial repaint during 01/02/18 works visit.

Fire damage at Dragoman 16/09/16.
Noted stored Express Service, Obraztsov Chiflik: 19/04/17 and 11/07/17. Subsequently repaired, with partial repaint.

Abbreviations:

Prepared at:	ETS: Electric Traction Services.
Works Codes:	**БЖК** : BZK/Koncar, **БК**: Koncar, Podujane, Sofia; EC: Express Service, Ruse; Reloc: Reloc SA, Craiova, Romania.
Liveries:	DRS: Direct Rail Services, NSE: Network South-East, LNW: London North-Western, BFY: Blue full yellow ends. OL: Orange safety line, NOL: No orange line, RNp: Red Nameplates.

Additional Notes:

87014 fitted with snow ploughs and bodyside access doors only prior to modification work being abandoned.
Allocation: Pirdop (ПИРдОП).

Full EVN Nos. were additionally applied circa August 2014.

87020, Sofia Koncar, 10 October 2009. Undergoing extensive modifications prior to entering service in Bulgaria.

87014, Sofia Koncar, 8 October 2011. This locomotive has never operated in Bulgaria.

Above left: **87013, Pirdop, 4 May 2011.**

Above right: **87013, Pirdop, 4 May 2011.** Works dates.

Below left: **87013, Pirdop, 4 May 2011.** Certification.

Below right: **87013, Pirdop, 8 September 2014.** EVN number.

87019, Bojchinovci, 5 October 2008. PTG 'The Great Bulgarian Track Bash' railtour. LNWR livery.

87012, Bobov Dol, 4 October 2009. PTG 'The Great Bulgarian Track Bash 2' railtour. NSE livery.

87006, Pirdop, 8 October 2009. DRS/First livery.

87008, 87022 and 87013, Pirdop, 15 October 2011. 87008 stored following copper theft (Cotswold livery); 87013/22 awaiting repairs.

87004 *Britannia*, **Pirdop, 15 October 2011.** BR Blue liveried *Britannia* stabled on a rake of sulphuric acid tanks at Pirdop. 87004 is the only named BZK Class 87 and also carries a cast BZK logo on the cab side beneath the driver's side windows.

87003, Koprivshtitsa, 6 October 2009. BZK dark green/yellow livery.

87006 and 87029, Pirdop, 6 October 2009. Awaiting departure to Razdelna (near Varna) with a rake of sulphuric acid tanks.

87028 and 87003, Pirdop, 6 October 2009. 'Riga' electric multiple-unit passing two Class 87s.

87003, Sofia, 1 May 2010. PTG 'Magnificent Seven to the Black Sea' railtour.

87004, Kazanlak, 3 May 2010. PTG 'Magnificent Seven to the Black Sea' railtour.

87004, Lakatnik, 6 May 2011. LCGB railtour.

87006, Septemvri, 7 October 2011. PTG 'The Great Bulgarian Track Bash 3' railtour.

87026, Vetovo, 5 May 2010. 'Pusher' locomotive on the daily Razdelna-Ruse Razpredelitelna service, predominantly serving the quarries at Senovo and Vetovo.

87012 and 87008, Karlovo, 7 May 2010. Razdelna-Pirdop discharged sulphuric acid tanks.

87028 and 401022, Klisura, 4 May 2011. Lead locomotives on an early evening Pirdop-Razdelna sulphuric acid tank train.

87033, Klisura, 4 May 2011. 'Pusher' locomotive on the same train.

87010, Klisura, 10 October 2011. Mixed cargo train from Razdelna to Pirdop entering one of the tunnels in the mountainous Klisura area.

87034, plus 87033 and 87019, Razdelna, 12 October 2011. BZK operated 87034 awaiting departure from Razdelna on the rear of the morning departure to Ruse Razpredelitelna. 87019 (in LNWR black livery) and 87033, the lead locomotives, can be seen in the distance.

87034, 87020, 87006 and 87010, Vetovo, 13 October 2011. Quadruple-header, including three locomotives with pantographs up!

87020, 87006 and 87010, plus 87034, Senovo, 13 October 2011. Down to a mere triple-header, with 87034 relegated to the rear of the train.

87022, Express Service, Ruse, 9 September 2014. Extensive repairs to 87022 were undertaken at Express Service following fire damage at Karnobat in December 2013. The dark blue livery was retained albeit without the large bodyside numbers.

87008, Express Service, Ruse, 9 August 2016. Stored, providing spares to other Class 87s; positioned on accommodation bogies.

87007, Pirdop, 19 September 2014. 87007, in Cotswold grey livery, stands at the head of rake of box wagons.

87022, between Pirdop and Anton, 6 July 2015. 'Pusher' locomotive on the early evening sulphuric acid tank train departure from Pirdop to Razdelna.

87012, Pirdop, 7 July 2015. 87012 in the repainted version of the Network South-East livery, on the rear of their signature traffic in Bulgaria i.e. sulphuric acid traffic (a by-product of copper refining) from Pirdop to Razdelna. 87012 is one of only four BZK locomotives to have been repainted during their time in Bulgaria, the others being 87004, 87019 and 87022. 87012 initially carried an incorrect EVN number; the incorrect '0' check-digit has, however, subsequently been changed to the correct '8'.

87007, 87026, 87020 and 87010, 87022, 87004, Pirdop, 7 July 2015. Stabled in the evening sunshine awaiting their next turns of duty.

87003 and 46026, Pirdop, 12 August 2016. 87003 alongside a recently repainted BDZ Class 46 (same Romanian-origin as the BZK-operated Class 40 locomotives). From October 2018, BDZ (the state railway operator) took over the Pirdop-Razdelna sulphuric acid and Burgas-Pirdop copper-ore flows from BZK, thereby significantly reducing the Class 87 workload in Bulgaria. BDZ deploy two of their Class 46 locomotives in top-and-tail mode.

87019, between Pirdop and Anton, 14 July 2017. Single-headed train of discharged sulphuric acid tanks shortly before arrival at Pirdop.

87009, 87007 and 87022, Obraztsov Chiflik, 18 April 2018. BZK meets Bulmarket (see Section 11).

87034, Express Service, Ruse, 18 April 2018. Carrying a slightly modified BZK livery following fire-damage repairs.

87014, Express Service, Ruse, 19 June 2019. After many years stored at Koncar, Sofia, and a short period at CERB, Sofia, 87014 has now taken up residence at the Express Service facility near Ruse. Visible behind 87014 are 87022, 87010, 87013 and 87006.

87004, Razdelna yard, 21 June 2019. Following repainting in July 2018, 87004 lost its cabside numbers, these being superceded by 12-digit EVN numbers on the cab fronts and bodysides.

11. Bulgaria: Bulmarket Class 86s and 87s

As mentioned previously, eleven Class 87s were rendered surplus when the BZK requirement was curtailed at seventeen locomotives. Seven of the eleven were scrapped but the remaining four in better condition (87009/17/23/25) were retained, with 87017/23 repainted in the Europhoenix livery for demonstration purposes. These locomotives, now owned by Europhoenix, eventually found a home with another Bulgarian private operator, this time Bulmarket (БУЛМАРКЕТ). These four were shipped on the *Oostvoorne* from Hull Docks on 1 November 2012 and discharged in Varna on the Black Sea on 29 November 2012; Class 86 86233 was shipped at the same time as a source of spares, more of which later.

The four Bulmarket 87s were sent to Koncar, Sofia, for refurbishment. Minimal work was required on 87017/23 following initial work undertaken by ETS (the engineering arm of Europhoenix) at Long Marston and their overhaul was completed by March 2013. 87009/25 were both exported in tatty Virgin livery and were originally thought by the railway enthusiast fraternity to be a source of spares; however, the ingenuity of the ETS, Koncar and Bulmarket engineers prevailed and both returned to traffic, although it took until February 2014 for 87025 to finally make it. The 'Bulgarianisation' work was exactly as per the BZK Class 87s, with the notable difference being the addition of a second pantograph.

87017/23 retained the blue/grey Europhoenix livery (with orange safety lines), albeit with the Europhoenix decals replaced by Bulmarket logos (in both Roman and Cyrillic alphabets); these two also retained their *Iron Duke* and *Velocity* nameplates. 87009/25 were reinstated to traffic with the simple but attractive Bulmarket red/black livery (without the orange safety lines).

The Bulmarket Class 87s can be seen widely across Bulgaria hauling liquid petroleum gas trains, with Ilyantsi, Ruse, Varna, Dolno Ezerovo and Belozem being good locations to see them in action. Being only a four-strong fleet, they are harder to track down than the more numerous BZK examples.

Bulmarket, always keen to acquire a good British asset, then turned their eyes to the Class 86s to further strengthen their fleet. 86233 (in Electric Blue livery) had already been acquired for spares for the Class 87s, and has lain dormant at Ruse Port since arrival. In April 2016, six Class 86s departed from Hull Docks on the *Hoogvliet* with discharge in Varna on 3 May 2016. Four locomotives were moved to the Express Service facility near Ruse for refurbishment, with two initially moving to Koncar, Sofia.

All six Class 86s were refurbished, even though 86231 and 86234 were originally thought to be for spares. Unlike the Class 87s before them, the Class 86s had to be renumbered to avoid any conflict with the ex-DSB (Danish State Railways) Class EA3000 locomotives operated (as 860xx) by both DB and Bulmarket in Bulgaria; as a consequence 86701, 86702, 86213 and 86235 were numbered 87701, 87702, 87703 and 87704 respectively. However, the Bulgarian railway authorities ultimately insisted on a separate number series to ensure that the Class 86s were clearly distinguishable from the Class 87s. Hence 87701-4 became 85001-4 during November/December 2016, with 86231 and 86234 subsequently following directly on as 85005 and 85006 respectively.

These six Class 86s had their headcode boxes removed as part of the refurbishment process, and were fitted with twin air pipes, two pantographs, modified headlight clusters, wing mirrors and snowploughs. All carry the latest version of the Bulmarket livery (i.e. grey and red) which was in fact heavily based around the ETL (Electric Traction Ltd) livery carried by 86702 when it arrived in Bulgaria, albeit with the yellow panels removed. Interestingly, 85002 (ex 86702) still carries the orange safety line at cantrail level indicating only a partial repaint in Bulgaria; the other five Class 86s received full repaints to replace their previous range of Anglia/Virgin/Colas Rail/InterCity liveries and, therefore, lost their orange lines. Full EVN numbers were positioned on the cab side (driver's side only), and, 5-digit numbers on the cab front (plus a check-digit for at least some of the four locomotives when numbered 87701-4); no locomotives with 8500x numbers have carried a check-digit on the cab front. As with the Class 87s, Bulmarket decals are carried in both Roman and Cyrillic alphabets.

86233 remains stored at Ruse although by 12 July 2017 it had managed to re-acquire some bogies, suggesting that some change of status may be in the pipeline.

Summary (Class 87):-

Loco No. Ex-UK EVN	Prepared at	Works Dates	Liveries/logos/names	Additional notes
87009 01/11/12 ex-Hull 91 52 00 **87 009**-4	Koncar, Sofia	БК: 31/07/13 EC: 07/07/16 EC: 30/10/18	Bulmarket NOL Bulmarketlogo (b+f) NNp	Repainted at Koncar, Sofia. ETH retained.
87017 01/11/12 ex-Hull 91 52 00 **87 017**-7	ETS Long Marston/ Koncar, Sofia	БК: 28/02/13 EC: 19/02/16 EC: 21/05/18	Europhoenix OL Bulmarketlogo (b+f) BNp ('*Iron Duke*')	ETH retained.
87023 01/11/12 ex-Hull 91 52 00 **87 023**-5	ETS Long Marston/ Koncar, Sofia	БК: 25/02/13 EC: 24/02/16 EC: 05/11/18	Europhoenix OL Bulmarketlogo (b+f) BNp ('*Velocity*')	ETH retained.
87025 01/11/12 ex-Hull 91 52 00 **87 025**-0	Koncar, Sofia	БК: 06/02/14 EC: 09/02/17 EC: 30/01/19	Bulmarket NOL Bulmarketlogo (b+f) NNp	Repainted at Koncar, Sofia. ETH retained.

Abbreviations:

Prepared at: ETS: Electric Traction Services.
Works Codes: БК: Koncar, Podujane, Sofia; EC: Express Service, Ruse.

Liveries: OL: Orange cantrail safety line; NOL: No orange line; BNp: Black nameplates; NNp: No nameplates.

Additional Notes:

87009/17/23/5 (plus 86233) loaded onto m.v. 'OOSTVOORNE' at Hull Docks on 01/11/12 and discharged at Varna, Bulgaria on 29/11/12; noted at Razdelna on 30/11/12.
87009/17/23/5 noted passing through Sofia station on 02/12/12 and at Koncar, Poduyane, Sofia on 04/01/13.

87009/17/23/5 modified with twin air pipes, twin pantographs, snow ploughs, wing mirrors, bodyside access panels, roof mounted headlights and roof mounted air horns.
EVN Nos. applied on release from Koncar, Sofia.

Allocation: Ruse Port Bulmarket (PYCE).

Summary (Class 85):-

BG Class 85 No./ EVN	BG Class 87 No./ EVN	UK No.	Ex-UK	Prepared at	Works Dates	Liveries/logos/names
85001 91 52 00 **85 001**-3	87701 91 52 00 **87 701**-6	86701	05/04/16 ex-Hull	EC	EC: 10/08/16	Bulmarket NOL Bulmarketlogo (b+f) RNp ('*Orion*')
85002 91 52 00 **85 002**-1	87702 91 52 00 **87 702**-4	86702	05/04/16 ex-Hull	EC	EC: 12/07/16 EC: 02/01/19	Bulmarket <u>OL</u> Bulmarketlogo (b+f) RNp ('*Cassiopeia*')
85003 91 52 00 **85 003**-9	87703 91 52 00 **87 703**-2	86213	05/04/16 ex-Hull	EC	EC: 06/10/16	Bulmarket NOL Bulmarketlogo (b+f) RNp ('*The Lancashire Witch*')
85004 91 52 00 **85 004**-7	87704 91 52 00 **87 704**-0	86235	05/04/16 ex-Hull	БК/EC	БК: 01/09/16	Bulmarket NOL Bulmarketlogo (b+f) RNp ('*Novelty*')
85005 91 52 00 **85 005**-4 -------	------- -------	86231	05/04/16 ex-Hull	EC	EC: 16/03/17 EC: 21/03/19	Bulmarket NOL Bulmarketlogo (b+f) RNp ('*Lady of the Lake*')
85006 91 52 00 **85 006**-2 -------	------- -------	86234	05/04/16 ex-Hull	БК/EC	EC: 16/08/17	Bulmarket NOL Bulmarketlogo (b+f) NNp

Noted Express Service, Obraztsov Chiflik: 18/10/18 (fire damage repairs). Returned to service.

| ------- ------- | ------- ------- | 86233 | 01/11/12 ex-Hull | ------- | ------- | EBSY OL NNp |

Noted stored: Ruse Port 06/07/13, 09/09/14, 02/09/15 and Ruse Port Quayside 10/08/16 (off-bogies), 20/04/17 (off-bogies), 12/07/17 (back on bogies). Source of spares.

Abbreviations:

Prepared at: БK: Koncar, Podujane, Sofia; EC: Express Service, Ruse.

Works Dates: As above.

Liveries: EBSY: Early Electric Blue with small yellow panels, OL: Orange cantrail safety line; NOL: No orange line, RNp: Red nameplates; NNp: No nameplates.

Logo positions: b: bodyside, f: front.

Additional Notes:

86233, with 87009/17/23/5, loaded onto m.v. 'OOSTVOORNE' at Hull on 01/11/12 and discharged at Varna, Bulgaria on 29/11/12; noted at Razdelna on 30/11/12.

86213/31/4/5, 86701/2 loaded onto m.v. 'HOOGVLIET' at Hull on 05/04/16 and discharged at Port of Varna West, Povelyanovo, Bulgaria on 03/05/16. All noted at Razdelna Yard on 03/05/16 (due to depart for Ruse 0300hrs 04/05/16).

86213/31, 86701/2 noted arriving at Express Service, Obraztsov Chiflik on 04/05/16 (ex Ruse). Noted again on 09/08/16 (86702 had already been out onto the main line for testing purposes and was awaiting acceptance; 86701 was undergoing testing).

86234/5 noted at Koncar, Sofia on 14/05/16 (already in workshop area) and 12/08/16 (under refurbishment). 86234/5 were subsequently transferred to Express Service, Obraztsov Chiflik for completion of work. (N.B. Some electrical work was undertaken on 86235 at Koncar). 86234 noted at Express Service on 19/04/17 (undergoing restoration).

86701/2, 86213/35 initially renumbered 87701-87704 respectively; subsequently re-classified Class 85 and renumbered to 85001-4 respectively. 86231/4 renumbered directly to 85005/6 respectively.
87701-4 (subsequently 85001-6) and 85005/6 were repainted at Express Service, Obraztsov Chiflik.

Allocation: Ruse Port Bulmarket (PYCE).

87017 and 87023, Long Marston, 18 September 2011. 'Europhoenix' livery.

87023, Long Marston, 5 May 2012. Preparatory work before export to Bulgaria.

87017, Varna Zapad, 4 September 2013. 'Europhoenix' livery retained but now with 'Bulmarket' decals (Cyrillic spelling on the front, Roman on the side). Between duties in Varna Zapad yard.

87025+55263, Belozem Oil Distribution Terminal, 13 September 2014. 87025 stabled between duties whilst Bulmarket Class 55 performs local shunting duties. Bulmarket red and black livery.

87023, Belozem, 14 September 2014. *Iron Duke* awaiting the 1600hrs departure time from Belozem, and the largely overnight journey to the Dolno Ezerovo refinery near Burgas.

87025, Belozem, 17 September 2014. 87025 in contrasting Bulmarket red and black livery stands in Belozem yard. The transformation carried out by Bulmarket, ETS and Koncar between this locomotive first arriving in Bulgaria in November 2012 and the completion of the refurbishment work in early 2014 was nothing less than astonishing.

87025, Port Bulmarket, Ruse, 12 July 2017. Stabling point and servicing depot.

37608 hauling 86213, 86702, 86701 and 86235 from Leicester to Barrow Hill at Clay Cross Jct, 30 March 2016. En route to Barrow Hill, then Hull, for a new life in Bulgaria.

86701, Barrow Hill, 31 March 2016. At Barrow Hill, the four recently arrived Class 86s were loaded onto Alleley's low-loaders for movement to Hull Docks for shipment to Varna, Bulgaria. At Hull, the four Barrow Hill Class 86s were joined by 86231 and 86234 from Long Marston.

86701, 86231, 86234, 86213, 86702 and 86235, near Razdelna, 3 May 2016. The six Class 86s during torrential rain in transit from Varna Port (Povelyanovo) to Razdelna hauled by BZK locomotive 92 53 0 81 0714-1 within hours of their arrival on Bulgarian soil.

86701, 86231, 86234, 86213, 86702 and 86235, Razdelna, 3 May 2016. Stabled in Razdelna yard.

86235, 86702, 86213, 86234, 86231, 86701, 87009 and 55182, Razdelna, 3 May 2016. Now in glorious sunshine, the six Class 86s are seen being shunted in Razdelna yard by Bulmarket locomotive 55182-0, making a spectacularly colourful line-up of motive power. Bulmarket 87009 appears in the consist.

87009, plus consist 86701, 86231, 86234, 86213, 86702 and 86235, Razdelna, 3 May 2016. Ready for overnight movement to Ruse (see also rear cover).

87025, 86003, 86702, 86213, 86231 and 86701, Obraztsov Chiflik, 4 May 2016. Bulmarket convoy and LPG train arriving from Ruse Razpredelitelna.

87009 plus 86701, 86231, 86213, 86702 and 86003, Obraztsov Chiflik 4 May 2016. 86701, 86231, 86213 and 86702 are seen being propelled towards the Express Service facility at Obraztsov Chiflik by Bulmarket 86003-4 (ex-DSB EA3003). 87009 waits patiently on the main line to assist with pushing the LPG train; on completion of shunting, 86003-4 formed the lead locomotive.

86003, 86702, 86213, 86231 and 86701, Obraztsov Chiflik, 4 May 2016. 86003-4 (ex-DSB EA3003) propelling the four Class 86s towards BZK Class 40 400553.

86702, 86213, 86231, 86701 and 400553, Obraztsov Chiflik, 4 May 2016. 86702 in ETS livery, which ultimately formed the basis of the livery for all six of the new arrivals.

87009, plus 400553, 86701, 86231, 86213 and 86702, with 87013 (in the distance), Obraztsov Chiflik, 4 May 2016.

86213, Express Service, Ruse, 9 August 2016. The transition begins for *The Lancashire Witch*.

86234, Koncar, Sofia, 12 August 2016. 86234 is seen inside the Koncar workshop with repairs underway; 86235 was also present at the time of this visit. Both locomotives were subsequently moved to the Express Service facility for completion of refurbishment work.

86702 Express Service Ruse 9 August 2016. '*Cassiopeia*' is complete apart from the application of its fleet number and is awaiting final acceptance. Modifications are clear, particularly the removal of the old headcode boxes, and the fitment of new light clusters, snow ploughs and two pantographs. This fifty year-old locomotive now looks brand new, with Bulmarket and Express Service bringing locomotive refurbishment to a whole new level of excellence!

87701 (86701), Kurilo (north of Sofia), 10 December 2016. The first four Class 86s were renumbered 87701-4 to avoid a clash with the Bulmarket/DB 860xx series locomotives (ex-DSB EA30xx). *(Miroslav Georgiev)*

85005 (86231), Express Service, Ruse, 19 April 2017. The Bulgarian railway authorities insisted on full numerical separation from the other (true) Class 87s in Bulgaria, and so 87701-4 were renumbered 85001-4; 85005 and 85006 appeared in this guise from the outset.

85003 (86213), Obraztsov Chiflik, 19 April 2017.

86233, Port Bulmarket, Ruse 12 July 2017. 86233 has resided at the Port of Ruse since arrival in Bulgaria. Nothing is wasted, though; various parts were recovered by Bulmarket to facilitate the transformation of the more recently arrived Class 86s. 86233 still carries the retro-Electric Blue livery applied during the latter days of its British career.

12. Bulgaria: DB Class 92s

ritish freight traffic operations have progressively been taken over by multi-national operators and/or operators with multinational aspirations; this has led to a pan-European appraisal of activities and the drive for more effective utilisation of assets. As a consequence, under utilised assets in one country have been increasingly moving to other countries for use within the same overall company. This approach has been deployed by DB (Deutsche Bahn).

The first DB Class 92 to move abroad was 92034 to Bulgaria in May 2012 under the auspices of DB Schenker Rail Bulgaria, followed by 92025/7 in December 2012, and 92030 in July 2015. All four locomotives retained their as-built double-grey livery, as well as the BR double-arrow logos, Crewe Electric depot diamonds and the Channel Tunnel roundels. The original 'transfer' names on 92025/7/34 were also retained; 92030 also carries an 'Ashford' transfer name, the previously fitted conventional nameplates having been removed prior to departure from the UK.

'Bulgarianisation' work was undertaken by Koncar, Sofia, this including the fitment of twin air pipes, wing mirrors, new protruding roof-mounted headlight, small snow ploughs and the Bulgarian signalling equipment. Class 92s were built from new with two pantographs.

All four Class 92s were 'allocated' to Pirdop and initially were heavily involved in the transportation of imported copper ore from the port of Burgas to the copper refinery at Pirdop, frequently operated in pairs, either with another Class 92 or with an ex-DSB (Danish State Railways) Class EA3000 (now series 86012-20). In mixed ex-DSB Class 86 and Class 92 pairings, the Class 92s were usually deployed as the lead locomotive, supporting the view that Co-Co traction is preferred given its superior adhesion performance. However, DB lost the copper ore contract at the end of December 2016, leaving the Class 92s short of work; the main traffic currently is copper ore from Chelopech to Burgas, and transit container traffic.

92022 arrived in Bulgaria in August 2017 and currently resides at Koncar, Sofia as a source of spares.

Current No./ EVN	First BG No./ EVN	UK No.	Ex-UK	Prepared at	Works Dates	Current liveries/logos/ names
------- -------	92022	92022	25/03/17 via Channel Tunnel	-	-	dgrfl EWSlogo ne/d Ooo NNp

Observations en route Bulgaria: Calais Fréthun (F): 02/04/17, Antwerpen Noord (B): 04/07/17, Curtici (RO): 27/08/17. Noted stored Pirdop (03/03/18, 21/04/18, 07/06/18). Used for spares. Transferred to Koncar, Sofia on 26/10/18. Noted stored at Koncar, Sofia (18/06/19).

Current No./ EVN	First BG No./ EVN	UK No.	Ex-UK	Prepared at	Works Dates	Current liveries/logos/ names
88025 91 52 16 **88025**-1	92025 91 70 00 **92025**-1	92025	01/12/12 via Channel Tunnel	СЕ/ БК	БК: 22/01/13 БК: 08/04/16	dgrfl DBlogo(b+f+rhc) ce CEd Ooo TNp (*Oscar Wilde*)

Observations en route Bulgaria: Aachen West (D): 03/12/12, Groenhart (Nürnberg-Treuchtlingen) (D): 13/12/12 (transit). First noted Koncar, Sofia: 02/01/13.

Current No./ EVN	First BG No./ EVN	UK No.	Ex-UK	Prepared at	Works Dates	Current liveries/logos/ names
88027 91 52 16 **88027**-7	92027 91 70 00 **92027**-7	92027	01/12/12 via Channel Tunnel	СЕ/ БК	БК: 22/01/13 БК: 27/01/16 БК: 05/03/19	dgrfl DBlogo(b+f+rhc) ce CEd Ooo TNp (*George Eliot*)

Observations en route Bulgaria: Aachen West (D): 03/12/12, Groenhart (Nürnberg-Treuchtlingen) (D): 13/12/12 (transit). First noted Koncar, Sofia: 02/01/13.

Current No./ EVN	First BG No./ EVN	UK No.	Ex-UK	Prepared at	Works Dates	Current liveries/logos/ names
88030 91 52 16 **88030**-1	92030 91 70 00 **92030**-1	92030	31/07/15 via Channel Tunnel	СЕ/БК	БК: 05/11/15 БК: 05/02/19	dgrfl DBlogo(b+f+rhc) ce CEd Ooo TNp (*Ashford*)

Observations en route Bulgaria: Calais Fréthun (F): 03/08/15, Hazebrouck (F): 03/08/15 (transit), Oisterwijk (NL): 04/08/15 (transit), Curtici (RO): 11/08/15 and 15/08/15, Sindel (BG): 210815 (transit), Pirdop (BG): 210815.

Current No./ EVN	First BG No./ EVN	UK No.	Ex-UK	Prepared at	Works Dates	Current liveries/logos/ names
88034 91 52 16 **88034**-3	92034 91 70 00 **92034**-3	92034	08-09/05/12 via Channel Tunnel	СЕ/ БК	БК: 16/06/12 БК: 16/06/15 БК: 26/10/18	dgrfl DBlogo(b+f+rhc) ce CEd Ooo TNp (*Kipling*)

Observations en route Bulgaria: Aachen West (D): 11/05/12, Duisburg Wedau (D): 25/05/12 (transit), Gelsenkirchen Bismark: 25/05/12, Mainz Kostheim: 25/05/12 (transit), Darmstadt-Kranichstein (D): 25/05/12, Curtici (RO): 29/05/12, Radulesti (RO): 01/06/12 (transit), Ruse (BG): 02/06/12. First noted Koncar, Sofia: 04/06/12.

Abbreviations:

Prepared at: CE: Crewe Electric Depot, **БК**: Koncar, Podujane, Sofia.

Livery details: dgrfl: Double-Grey Railfreight livery, ce: Cabside BR double-arrow emblem, CEd: Crewe Electric depot diamond plate,
Ooo: Channel Tunnel roundels,
TNp: Transfer nameplates, NNp: No nameplates.

Logo position: b: bodyside, f: front, rhc: right-hand cab side.

Additional Notes:

92025/7/30/4 modified with twin air pipes, wing mirrors, protruding roof mounted headlights and small snow ploughs.

Unlike the BZK Class 87s, 92025/7/34 did not carry check-digits with their numbers when initially introduced in Bulgaria; EVN numbers were applied from about March 2015. 92030 entered traffic in Bulgaria with EVN numbers.

92025/7/34 entered traffic still carrying the large EWS logos on their bodysides. Subsequently changed to diminutive DB logos: 92025 (July/August 2016), 92027 (November/December 2015), and 92034 (by 27/05/16 after a short period with no bodyside logos at all). It is believed that 92030 entered traffic in Bulgaria with bodyside DB logos.

92025/7/30/4 were re-numbered to 88025/7/30/4 during March/April 2017.

Allocation: Pirdop (ПИРдОП).

92034 and 92025, Burgas, 12 September 2014. The DB Class 92s operated initially without EVN numbers.

92025, Dolno Ezerovo, 16 September 2014. *Oscar Wilde* looped at Dolno Ezerovo station whilst hauling a rake of nine empty six-axled bogie copper-ore wagons from Pirdop to Burgas.

92025, Dolno Ezerovo, 16 September 2014. Not too much modification since leaving the UK, but the wing mirrors, modified roof headlights and snow ploughs are clear evidence of its new Bulgarian sphere of operation. The BR 'double-arrow' logo, Channel Tunnel roundels, '*Oscar Wilde*' name and Crewe Electric depot diamonds are all retained!

92025, Burgas, 16 September 2014. Empty copper-ore wagons returning to Chelopech.

232613 and 92027, Balgarovo, 8 July 2015. An interesting combination of Russian and British motive power.

92034, Balgarovo, 9 July 2015. '*Kipling*' passes through Balgarovo on the last part of its journey from Pirdop to Burgas conveying a mixture of four and six axle empty copper- ore wagons. EVN numbers applied.

92030, Balgarovo, 11 August 2016. DB logos have finally replaced the EWS 'three-beasties'.

88030 and 88034, Pirdop, 10 July 2017. Now renumbered into the 880xx series to comply with Bulgarian railway requirements.

88025 and 88034, Pirdop, 18 June 2019. Stabled in the Deutsche Bahn sidings awaiting their next turn of duty.

92022, Koncar, Sofia, 18 June 2019. Spares donor locomotive, with many components already removed including a bogie exchange with 92027 (88027).

13. Hungary: Floyd Class 56s and 86s

Between the Bulgarian BZK and Bulmarket Class 87 sales, Europhoenix sold eight Class 86s, previously purchased from HSBC, to private-operator Floyd ZRt in Hungary. These eight were heavily refurbished by ETS at Long Marston, this including the removal of the headcode boxes and the fitment of modified light-clusters and wider pantographs. They were exported to Hungary, via Immingham, between February 2009 and July 2013. The EVM-102 signalling system, together with other local necessities, were fitted on arrival in Hungary. The locomotives were numbered in the series 450 001 to 450 008.

The first six locomotives were given an all-over black livery with a pink waist-line stripe and Floyd logos. The 'Pink Floyd' pseudonym was inevitable! With the acquisition of Floyd ZRt by Eurogate International in 2013, some livery modifications were applied, with the pink stripe replaced by a half red/half-blue stripe; revised Floyd logos were also applied. The last two locomotives of the operational fleet were delivered in this revised livery, with the first six locomotives retrospectively modified to match. The class is currently in the throes of being further altered by the addition of a white bodyside panel above waist level and between the cab doors; 450 001/2/4-8 have so far received this livery revision.

86424, numbered 450 009 and still in all-over Network Rail yellow livery, subsequently arrived in Hungary during August 2013 initially as a source of spares, based at Budapest Keleti. In 2017 Floyd authorised repairs to 86424 and work commenced at Keleti to secure a reinstatement to traffic. By mid-October 2018 the overhaul of 86424 (now in Floyd(v3) livery) was largely complete. 'Designated Body' inspection and authorisation examinations were undertaken on 7 November 2018, with final 'tweaking' and cosmetic attention continuing into early-2019. Although not confirmed, entry into traffic was expected by April 2019.

450 005 to 008 were despatched from the UK fitted with twin pantographs, an operational insurance preferred by Eastern European operators. 450 001 to 450 004 are still operating with a single pantograph.

Floyd has also taken delivery of three Class 56s from Europhoenix, two delivered in operational condition. 56101 (659 001) and 56115 (659 002) were exported in June and September 2012 respectively via Immingham Docks after preparation at Nemesis, Burton, both in black livery with pink stripe. The two subsequent livery modifications, as per the Floyd Class 86s, have also been applied to the Class 56s. 56117 (still in French Fertis livery) was exported from the UK in July 2013 as a source of spares. This locomotive resides at Budapest Keleti.

Both the Floyd Class 86s and 56s operate a variety of traffic across Hungary, much of it spot-hire work. The Budapest-Hegyeshalom corridor is probably the richest vein for seeing these locomotives in action.

Summary (Class 86):

Loco No./EVN Current front-end No.	Ex B.R. No.	Prepared At	Ex-UK	Liveries/logos (with first and last seen)	Details
91 55 0450 001-7 91 55 0450 001-7	86248	ETS Long Marston	10/02/09 ex-Immingham	Floyd(v1) Floydlogo(v1)(b+f) (last 10/07/13) Floyd(v2) Floydlogo(v2)(b+f) (first 31/08/13, last 08/06/18) Floyd(v3) Floydlogo(v2)(b+f) (first 23/01/19)	NHL, WWR, SFP(x1).

Noted en route: Cuxhaven-Hamburg (D): 12/02/09 (transit). Originally delivered with 0450 001-7 front-end number.
Noted Budapest Keleti depot: 08/06/18 (being repainted into Floyd (v3) livery) and 23/01/19 (repainting complete).

Loco No./EVN Current front-end No.	Ex B.R. No.	Prepared At	Ex-UK	Liveries/logos (with first and last seen)	Details
91 55 0450 002-5 450 002	86250	ETS Long Marston	31/05/09 ex-Immingham	Floyd(v1) Floydlogo(v1)(b+f) (last 15/06/13) Floyd(v2) Floydlogo(v2)(b+f) (first 31/08/13, last 17/01/14) Floyd(v3) Floydlogo(v2)(b+f) (first 07/07/14)	NHL, NWWR, SFP(x1),

Originally delivered with 0450 002-5 front-end number.
Substantially rebuilt cab including new driver's desk, air-conditioning, and removal of partitions.

Loco No./EVN Current front-end No.	Ex B.R. No.	Prepared At	Ex-UK	Liveries/logos (with first and last seen)	Details
91 55 0450 003-3 450 003-3	86232	ETS Long Marston	20/04/10 ex-Immingham	Floyd(v1) Floydlogo(v1)(b+f) (last 05/09/13) Floyd(v2) Floydlogo(v2)(b+f) (first 03/10/13, last 03/06/18)	NHL, NWWR, SFP(x1).
91 55 0450 004-1 0450 004-1	86218	ETS Long Marston	22/02/11 ex-Immingham	Floyd(v1) Floydlogo(v1)(b+f) (last 05/09/13) Floyd(v2) Floydlogo(v2)(b+f) (first 21/09/13, last 05/06/14) Floyd(v3) Floydlogo(v2)(b+f) (first 19/07/14)	NHL/BSL, WWR, SFP(x1).

Noted en route: Hamburg Harburg (D): 26/02/11 and 27/02/11.

Loco No./EVN Current front-end No.	Ex B.R. No.	Prepared At	Ex-UK	Liveries/logos (with first and last seen)	Details
91 55 0450 005-8 450 005	86215	ETS Long Marston	21/05/12 ex-Immingham	Floyd(v1) Floydlogo(v1)(b+f) (last 17/07/13) Floyd(v2) Floydlogo(v2)(b+f) (first 10/08/13, last 02/03/16) Floyd(v3) Floydlogo(v2)(b+f) (first 05/11/16)	NHL, NWWR, SFP(x2).

Noted en route: Hamburg Harburg (D): 01/06/12 and 03/06/12.

| 91 55 0450 006-6 450 006 | 86217 | ETS Long Marston | 11/02/13 ex-Immingham | Floyd(v1) Floydlogo(v1)(b+f) (last 15/06/13) Floyd(v2) Floydlogo(v2)(b+f) (first 01/10/13, last 02/10/14) Floyd(v3) Floydlogo(v2)(b+f) (first 14/11/14) | NHL, NWWR, SFP(x2). |

Noted en route: Bottrop-Welheim (D): 16/02/13 (transit), Duisburg (D): 16/02/13 (transit), Himberg (D): 17/02/13 (transit), Hegyeshalom (HU): 17/02/13.

| 91 55 0450 007-4 450 007 | 86228 | ETS Long Marston | 07/07/13 ex-Imminghams | Floyd(v2) Floydlogo(v2)(b+f) (last 09/08/14) Floyd(v3) Floydlogo(v2)(b+f) (first 06/10/14) | NHL, NWWR, SFP(x2). |

Noted en route: Hamburg Harburg (D): 13/07/13, Münster (D): 13/07/13 (transit), Krefeld-Linn (D): 14/07/13.

| 91 55 0450 008-2 450 008 | 86242 | ETS Long Marston | 07/07/13 ex-Immingham | Floyd(v2) Floydlogo(v2)(b+f) (last 12/09/14) Floyd(v3) Floydlogo(v2)(b+f) (first 14/11/14) | NHL, WWR, SFP(x2). |

Noted en route: Hamburg Harburg (D): 13/07/13, Münster (D): 13/07/13 (transit), Krefeld-Linn (D): 14/07/13.

| 91 55 0450 009-0 ------- | 86424 | Budapest Keleti | 08/08/13 ex-Immingham | NR NRlogo (last 08/06/18) Floyd(v3) Floydlogo(v2)(b) (first 18/10/18) | NHL, NWWR, SFP(x1) |

Noted en route: Bremervörde (D): 22/08/13, Lemförde (D): 24/08/13 (transit), Krefeld-Linn (D): 25/08/13, Lintorf (D): 28/08/13 (transit), XX (HU): 29/08/13 (transit).

Noted Budapest Keleti: 07/10/13 (stored, accommodation bogies).

Noted Budapest Keleti being rebuilt: 04/11/17 (accommodation bogies), 08/06/18 (accommodation bogies) and 18/10/18 (repairs almost complete, refurbished Class 86 bogies, repainted).

Designated Body' inspection/authorisation examinations undertaken on 07/11/18; noted at Budapest Ferencváros with 450 008 (86242) for insurance on this date.

Noted Budapest Keleti 23/01/19 prior to entering revenue earning service.

Summary (Class 56):

Loco No./EVN Front-end No.	Ex B.R. No.	Prepared At	Ex-UK	Liveries/logos (with first and last dates seen)	Details
92 55 0659 001-5 0659 001-5	56101	**Nemesis, Burton**	**06/06/12 ex-Immingham**	**Floyd(v1) Floydlogo(v1) (b) (last 20/07/13) Floyd(v2) Floydlogo(v2)(b) (first 03/09/13, last 18/04/14) Floyd(v3) Floydlogo(v2)(b) (first 17/06/14)**	NHL

Noted en route: Cuxhaven (D): 14/06/12, Hamburg Harburg (D): 15/06/12, Budapest Soruksari Út (HU): 18/06/12.

Loco No./EVN Front-end No.	Ex B.R. No.	Prepared At	Ex-UK	Liveries/logos (with first and last dates seen)	Details
92 55 0659 002-3 659 002	56115	**Nemesis, Burton**	**12/09/12 ex-Immingham**	**Floyd(v1) Floydlogo(v1)(b) (last 05/09/13) Floyd(v2) Floydlogo(v2)(b) (first 23/09/13, last 13/07/14) Floyd(v3) Floydlogo(v2)(b) (first 01/09/14)**	NHL

Noted en route: Hamburg Harburg (D): 19/09/12, Eisenach (D): 29/09/12, Gotha (D): 30/09/12, Klostermansfeld-Benndorf (D): 03/10/12, XX (D): 21/10/12.

On 28/11/16, 56115, whilst hauling a loaded tank train, was involved in an accident at Nyúl near Győr (on the Győr-Veszprém line); it collided with a lorry that had failed to stop at an ungated crossing, crushing the locomotive's No.2 cab. The driver was unfortunately killed in the incident. Subsequently moved to Budapest Keleti for repairs.

Noted 22/05/17 having last parts of damaged cab removed, and, 26/05/17 having damaged cab framework repaired.

Noted 04/11/17 with cab ex-56106 fitted and body being rubbed down ready for repainting. MW cables and receptacles removed; receptacle positions plated over.

Noted 15/01/18 at Budaörs in ex-works condition. Original front-end number, 0659 002-3, replaced by 659 002.

Loco No./EVN Front-end No.	Ex B.R. No.	Prepared At	Ex-UK	Liveries/logos (with first and last dates seen)	Details
92 55 0659 003-1 0659 003-1	56117	-------	**13/07/13 ex-Immingham**	**Fertis Fertislogo(b+lhc)**	SL

Noted en route: Bremervörde (D): 22/08/13, Lemförde (D): 24/08/13 (transit), Krefeld-Linn (D): 25/08/13, Lintorf (D): 28/08/13 (transit), XX (HU): 29/08/13 (transit).

Never used in Hungary. Noted stored Budapest Keleti: 07/10/13, 26/05/17, 08/06/18, 23/01/19 (source of spares).

Abbreviations:

Liveries:
Floyd(v1): All-over black livery, pink waist stripe,
Floyd(v2): All-over black livery, ½ red /½blue stripe,
Floyd(v3): Black livery with white upper bodyside area between cab doors, ½ red /½blue stripe.

Logos:
Floydlogo(v1): FLOYD bodyside lettering,
Floydlogo(v2): *FLOYD* lettering within red/blue circle, plus 'Railway for the future' signage.

Logo positions: b: bodyside, f: front.

Details:
SL: British spotlight, BSL: Old British box-style headlight below front cab windows, NHL: New Hungarian-style headlight replacing British spotlight
WWR/NWWR: Windscreen wiper 'recess' / No 'recess';
SFP(x1) or (x2): Stone-Faiveley Pantograph (1 or 2 pantographs fitted).

56101 (659 001-5), Győrszentiván, 8 October 2012. 659 001-5 (56101) awaits the road at Győrszentiván with a substantial trainload of coke from Dunaújváros (Hungary) to Pont à Mousson (France), which 56101 hauled as far as Hegyeshalom on the Austrian/Hungarian border.

56101 (659 001-5), Győr, 8 October 2012. Same train at Győr.

240088 and 56101 (659 001-5), Győr, 8 October 2012. 659 001-5 (56101) waiting time, alongside Slovak "Laminate" 240 088-5 on a car train. 56101 exhibits the original Floyd(v1) livery with pink stripe.

56101 (659 001-5), Gonyu Port, 13 October 2012. Mercia Charters 'The Pre-Emptive Strike' railtour.

56115 (659 002-3), Dunaújváros Kikoto, 5 October 2013. Floyd(v2) livery with revised bodyside stripe colours and logos. Mercia Charters 'The Things Past' railtour.

56115 (659 002-3), Budapest Keleti, 5 October 2013. The Mercia Charters railtour on return to Budapest.

56101 (659 001-5), Budapest Keleti, 7 October 2013. 659 001-5 on the turntable at Keleti depot illustrating the second variation of the Floyd i.e. half red/half blue stripe with revised Floyd decals.

56117 (659 003-1), Budapest Keleti, 7 October 2013. 56117, providing spares for 56101/15, in Fertis livery reflecting its previous excursion to France.

56115 (659 002-3), Budapest Keleti, 26 May 2017. Third version of the Floyd livery with the painting of the top half of the bodyside between the cabs in white. At the time it was suggested that this white repainting was an effort to reduce the propensity for Class 56s to overheat; however, the application of white to the Class 86s as well leaves this notion open to question! No.2 cab removed following accident damage near Nyúl in November 2016.

56115 (659 002-3), Budapest Keleti, 4 November 2017. New cab fitted from 56106; 56115 re-entered traffic in early 2018.

86217, Long Marston, 5 May 2012. Extensive preparatory work being undertaken by ETS prior to export to Hungary.

86242, 86228, 86702 and 86701, hauled by 56312, Chesterfield, 4 July 2013. 86228 and 86242, as 450 007 and 008 respectively, en route to Barrow Hill ready for loading onto road transport for movement to Immingham Docks. 86701 and 86702 had to a wait a further three years to emigrate to Eastern Europe.

86215 (450 005-8), Hidasnémeti, 11 October 2012. Floyd(v1) livery. 86215 (450 005-8) clearly shows the two pantograph configuration with which 450 005 to 450 008 were delivered.

751 113, 630 030 and 86215 (450 005-8), Hidasnémeti, 11 October 2012. Floyd-operated 86215 on a train of coke at Hidasnémeti, Hungary near the Slovak Republic border awaiting departure, keeping company with Slovak and Hungarian motive power. The coke train originated in Poland and is destined for Romania; the Class 86 worked the train from Hidasnémeti to Debrecen via Felsözsölca.

86215 (450 005-8), Encs, 11 October 2012.

86250(450 002-5) and 86424(450 009-0), Budapest Keleti, 7 October 2013. Floyd(v2) livery. 86250 (450 002-5) undergoing maintenance repair work in Budapest Keleti depot alongside 86424 (450 009-0) which at that time was acting as a source of spares. 86250 was in the process of transitioning from the original pink-stripe Floyd livery to the red/blue stripe version, whilst 86424 retains the Network Rail all-over yellow scheme.

86242 (450 008-2) and 86424 (450 009-0), Budapest Keleti, 4 November 2017. 86424 showing signs of a return to traffic despite earlier expectations of spares donorship only.

86248 (450 001-7), 86242 (450 008-2) and 86218 (450 004-1), Soruksari Út, 22 May 2017. Between duties on the outskirts of Budapest.

86228 (450 007-4), 230067 and 242271, Hegyeshalom, 28 May 2017. Floyd(v3) livery. Multi-national traction on the Austrian/Hungarian border.

86250 (450 002-5), Hegyeshalom, 28 May 2017. Note the Hungarian signalling equipment below the buffer beam.

86424 (450 009-0), Budapest Keleti, 23 January 2019. Rebuilding almost complete and following a Designated Body inspection on 7 November 2018, 450 009-0 undergoes final modifications at Keleti depot prior to introduction into revenue-earning service. Major modifications included significant transformer cooling improvements, cab up-grading and the installation of cameras for driver rear-viewing.

86217 (450 006-6), Budapest Keleti, 22 January 2019. Turntable manoevring – a rare occurrence for a Class 86 in the United Kingdom, but relatively common in Hungary.

14. Hungary: CRS Class 47

Despite being the most numerous mainline British locomotive class and also equipped with a Sulzer engine (common in Eastern Europe), perhaps the strangest British export in many ways has been 47375. This left the UK in October 2015 for a new life in Hungary with Continental Railway Solution (CRS), after preparation (including the removal of headcode boxes and fitment of new light clusters) and repainting at Nemesis, Burton. After a protracted stop-over in Rotterdam, it finally arrived in Hungary in April 2016. Hungarian signalling equipment and wing mirrors were fitted on arrival in Hungary.

47375 gained full accreditation for operation on the Hungarian railway system on 26 May 2017, the day before it entered revenue-earning service in Hungary with an enthusiast railtour.

During 2018, 47375 was leased back to Nemesis Rail and is expected to be fully engaged over the next two years on engineering trains across Hungary.

Summary:

Loco No./EVN Front-end No.	Ex B.R. No.	Prepared At	Ex-UK	Livery/logo/name	Details
92 70 0047 375-5 047-375	47375	**Nemesis, Burton**	05/10/15 ex-Hull	**CRS CRSlogo StNp ('*FALCON*')**	**NLC, WM**

Noted Rotterdam Europoort: 06/10/15+13/04/16.

Noted en route: Valburg (NL): 13/04/16 (transit), xx(D): 13/04/16 (transit), Linz (A): 14/04/16, Zurndorf (A): 14/04/16 (transit), Budapest (HU): 15/04/16.

Named '*FALCON*' on 06/10/16 at Budapest Nyugati station.

Noted on test at Kőbánya-Kispest on 13-14/11/16.

CRS railtour duties on 27/05/17, and, 09-10/06/18 (from Budapest to Mürzzuschlag (A)).

Abbreviations:

Detail differences: NLC: New light clusters; WM: Wing mirrors.

Livery: StNp: 'Stencilled' names.

47375, Budapest Ferencváros, 26 May 2017. Pre-railtour re-fuelling.

47375 and 242274, Rákos, 26 May 2017. The sublime and the ridiculous! TranslogSlovakia Škoda Class 242 in a, somewhat, garish livery and 47375 in more traditional-style in the process of picking up the coaching stock for the CRS railtour the following day.

47375, Budapest Nyugati, 27 May 2017. CRS railtour at Budapest prior to departure on a circular excursion around Hungary including Rétszilas and Komarom.

47375 and 044112, Komárom, 27 May 2017. CRS railtour locomotive run-round passing a Škoda locomotive in a slightly more conservative livery, but the Class 47 steals the show!

47375, Mürzzuschlag, 10 June 2018. On 9 June 2018 47375 was deployed on an enthusiast special from Budapest Keleti to Mürzzuschlag (Austria), via Wiener Neustadt, reaching an altitude of 895m at Semmering. The special returned to Budapest late afternoon on 10 June. During much of the Sunday 47375 was an exhibit at the Südbahn Open Day at Mürzzuschlag alongside steam, diesel and electric motive power from Austria, Hungary and Slovenia. The Open Day celebrated the 20th anniversary of the Semmering line achieving UNESCO World Heritage Site status. In this photograph, 47375 keeps company with ex-ÖBB electric 1010.02 which earlier in the day had arrived on a special train with 2-6-4 steam locomotive 310.23.

47375, Mürzzuschlag, 10 June 2018. Two distinctively different designs, with 47375 positioned with NOHAB diesel M61.001 which had arrived on another special from Hungary with 4-8-0 steam locomotive 424.247.

15. Romania: DB Class 92s

The movement of DB Class 92s to Romania commenced with 92012 in May 2013, followed by 92001 in July 2013. After a gap, 92002/24 departed the UK in April 2015 followed by 92005/39 in May 2015 (although the latter two spent some considerable time in Calais pending resolution of 'transit issues'). 'Romanianisation' took place at the Softronic workshops in Craiova, including the fitment of twin air pipes, wing mirrors and the Romanian signalling equipment. At the same time, locomotives were repainted in the DB red livery, although the BR double-arrow logos, Crewe Electric (CE) diamonds, and Channel Tunnel roundels were retained, the exception being 92001 which had its BR and CE logos removed in the UK at the time of its repaint into EWS livery. Locomotives were renumbered into the series 472 001 to 472 006.

The Class 92s in Romania were exclusively deployed on freight trains. The principal route on which the locomotives were used was the west-to-east corridor from Curtici (near the Hungarian border) to Constanţa (on the Black Sea coast) via Arad, Simeria, Târgu Jiu, Craiova, Caracal, Bucureşti and Feteşti. However, the Class 92s could also be found on a number of other routes e.g. Bucureşti to Braşov (via Ploeşti), Braşov to Constanţa (via Ploeşti, Buzău and Ţăndărei), etc. The Class 92s worked turn and turn about with other locomotives within the DB fleet, namely Classes 470 and 480 ('*Transmontana*') locomotives, with extensive night time operations.

92003 and 92026 arrived in Romania in May 2017 as sources of spares.

The Class 92s appear to have been well regarded by DB Romania although they were apparently relatively expensive to maintain compared with the indigenous locomotives within the DB fleet. The referendum vote for the UK to leave the EU and the impact that this has had on the value of the pound will have exacerbated the problem further and may well have triggered a decision to sell the Class 92 fleet to Russian company LocoTech in late-2017 for deployment by Transagent Špedicija in Croatia.

After preparatory work at Turceni, 472 001/003-005 were transferred to Croatia between November 2017 and July 2018. It is believed that 472 002 and 472 006 together with 92003/26 (after full rehabilitation) were due to follow, but that the contract with LocoTech was ultimately curtailed after four locomotives.

472 002 and 472 006 continue to work in Romania, and have now been joined in traffic by both 472 007 (92003) and 472 008 (92026). Although mechanically and electrically fully refurbished, 472 007 and 472 008 still retain their two-tone grey livery, at least for the time being.

Summary (operational locomotives):-

Loco No./EVN	UK No.	Ex-UK	Prepared at (with completion date)	Liveries/logos	Names
91 53 0 472 001-3	92012	08/05/13	Softronic, Craiova (09/13)	DB DBlogo (b+f) ce CEd Ooo bn+fn	TNp (*Mihai Eminescu*) (below roundels)

Observations en route Romania: Mattenmühle (D): 22/05/13, Augsberg (D): 27/05/13 and 14/06/13, Kelenfold (HU): 06/07/13, Szolnok (HU): 07/07/13, Békéscsaba (HU): 08/07/13.
Noted Softronic, Craiova (RO): 13/09/13 (DB livery).
Trade exhibit: Băneasa, Bucureşti (RO), 09-10/10/13.
Transferred to Croatia: 05/07/18 (ex-Turceni, Romania: 02/07/18).

Loco No./EVN	UK No.	Ex-UK	Prepared at (with completion date)	Liveries/logos	Names
91 53 0 472 002-1	92001	11/07/13	Softronic, Craiova (10/13)	DB DBlogo (b+f) ne/d Ooo bn+fn	TNp (*Mircea Eliade*) (above roundels)

Observations en route Romania: Albertirsa (nr Cegléd) (HU) : 09/09/13,
Noted: Softronic, Craiova (RO): 27/10/13.
Trade exhibit: Bucureşti Nord (RO), 10-17/06/14.

Loco No./EVN	UK No.	Ex-UK	Prepared at (with completion date)	Liveries/logos	Names
91 53 0 472 003-9	92002	10/04/15	Softronic, Craiova (07/15)	DB DBlogo (b+f) ce CEd Ooo cn+fn	TNp (*Lucian Blaga*) (below roundels)

Observations en route Romania: Calais Fréthun: 15/04/15, Hazebrouck (F): 18/04/15 (transit), Muizen (B): 21/04/15 and 25/04/15, Rotselaar (B): 25/04/15 (transit), Neuss (D): 25/04/15, St.Valentin (A): 15/05/15 (transit), Hegyeshalom (HU): 16/05/15, Budapest Kelenfold (HU): 16/05/15, Line 120 (HU): 17/05/15 (transit), Curtici (RO): 19/05/15.
Transferred to Croatia: 18/03/18 (ex-Turceni, Romania: 09/03/18).

Loco No./EVN	UK No.	Ex-UK	Prepared at (with completion date)	Liveries/logos	Names
91 53 0 472 004-7	92024	10/04/15	Softronic, Craiova (07/15)	DB DBlogo (b+f) ce CEd Ooo bn+fn	TNp (*Marin Preda*) (below roundels)

Observations en route Romania: Calais Fréthun: 15/04/15, Hazebrouck (F): 18/04/15 (transit), Muizen (B): 21/04/15 and 25/04/15, Rotselaar (B): 25/04/15 (transit), Neuss (D): 25/04/15, St.Valentin (A): 15/05/15 (transit), Hegyeshalom (HU): 16/05/15, Budapest Kelenfold (HU): 16/05/15, Line 120 (HU): 17/05/15 (transit), Curtici (RO): 19/05/15.
Transferred to Croatia: 05/07/18 (ex-Turceni, Romania: 02/07/18).

Loco No./EVN	UK No.	Ex-UK	Prepared at (with completion date)	Liveries/logos	Names
91 53 0 472 005-4	92005	29/05/15	Softronic, Craiova (10/15)	DB DBlogo (b+f) ce CEd Ooo cn+fn	TNp (*Emil Cioran*) (below roundels)

Observations en route Romania: Calais Fréthun (F): 29/05/15+03/08/15, Hazebrouck (F): 03/08/15 (transit), Oisterwijk (NL): 04/08/15 (transit), Curtici (RO): 11/08/15 and 15/08/15.
Noted Curtici (RO): 09/11/15 (ex-works).
Noted Turceni (RO): 26/09/17 and 27/09/17 (being prepared for Croatia).
Transferred to Croatia: 20/11/17 (ex-Turceni, Romania: 09/11/17).

Loco No./EVN	UK No.	Ex-UK	Prepared at (with completion date)	Liveries/logos	Names
91 53 0 472 006-2	**92039**	**29/05/15**	**Softronic, Craiova (01/16)**	**DB DBlogo (b+f) ce CEd Ooo bn+fn**	**TNp (*Eugen Ionescu*)** (below roundels)

Observations en route Romania: Calais Fréthun (F): 29/05/15+03/08/15, Hazebrouck (F): 15/11/15 (transit), Staple (F): 15/11/15 (transit), Kijfhoek (NL): 17/11/15+24/11/15.
Noted Arad (RO): 08/03/16 (repainted).

Summary (stored locomotives):-

91 53 0 472 007-0	**92003**	**25/03/17**	**DB Turceni (04/19)**	**dgrfl EWSlogo ce CEd Ooo**	**TNp (*Beethoven*)**

Observations en route Romania: Calais Fréthun (F): 02/04/17, La Madeleine (Tourcoing) (F): 12/04/17 (transit), Lauwe (Mouscron-Kortrijk) (B): 12/04/17 (transit), Antwerpen Noord: 18/04/17+29/04/17, Budapest Kelenfold (HU): 10/05/17, Curtici (RO): 12/05/17.
Noted stored Turceni (RO): 26/09/17+14/01/18 (providing spares) and 22/05/18 (undergoing repairs).
After rehabilitation, entered traffic in Romania on 24/04/19.

91 53 0 472 008-8	**92026**	**25/03/17**	**DB Turceni (07/19)**	**dgrfl EWSlogo ce CEd Ooo**	**TNp (*Britten*)**

Observations en route Romania: Calais Fréthun (F): 02/04/17, La Madeleine (Tourcoing) (F): 12/04/17 (transit), Lauwe (Mouscron-Kortrijk) (B): 12/04/17 (transit), Antwerpen Noord: 18/04/17+29/04/17, Budapest Kelenfold (HU): 10/05/17, Curtici (RO): 12/05/17.
Noted stored Turceni (RO): 26/09/17+14/01/18 (providing spares; accommodation bogies) and 22/05/18 (undergoing repairs, accommodation bogies).
After rehabilitation, entered traffic in Romania on 05/07/19.

Abbreviations:

Livery details: dgrfl: Double-Grey Railfreight livery, ce: Cabside BR double-arrow emblem, CEd: Crewe Electric depot diamond plate, Ooo: Channel Tunnel roundels,
cn: cabside numbers, bn: bodyside numbers, fn: front-end numbers; TNp: Transfer names.

Logo position: b: bodyside, f: front.

92002 (472 003-9), Turceni, 7 September 2015. *Lucian Blaga* in ex-works condition following very recent attention at Softronic in Craiova, including a repaint into DB red livery. Retention of the BR double-arrow emblem, the Crewe Electric depot diamonds and the Channel Tunnel roundels contrasts with the newly applied DB livery.

92001 (472 002-1), Caracal, 9 September 2015. *Mercia Eliade* awaits the road with a container train at Caracal. This is on the 600-mile arterial route between Curtici and Constanţa via Bucureşti.

92001 (472 002-1) and 480 011, Videle, 9 September 2015. Awaiting the road again at Videle and now with Softronic 'Transmontana' locomotive 91 53 0 480 011-2 for company, 472 002-1 stands in the late evening sun with a liner train gradually making its way towards București.

92005 (472 005-4), Timişoara, 19 June 2016. Portrait of *Emil Cioran* which became the first of the Romanian fleet to move to Croatia for further use with Transagent Rail.

92024 (472 004-7), Simeria, 20 June 2016. *Marin Preda* passing Simeria with a long rake of vans heading west towards Arad/Curtici.

92024 (472 004-7), Turceni, 22 June 2016. 92024 carefully manoevres through the catenary and vegetation in Turceni yard; slightly different from Wembley Yard!

92026, Turceni, 22 May 2018. 92026 has relinquished its bogies and now resides on accommodation bogies. Bogies, refurbished by Express Service, Ruse, were ready in the adjacent workshop for fitment as part of the refurbishment repairs.

92003, Turceni, 22 May 2018. 92003 and 92026 were originally transferred to Romania as sources of spares. However, after extensive repairs, 92003 entered revenue-earning service in Romania on 24 April 2019, followed by 92026 on 5 July 2019.

16. Croatia: LocoTech/Transagent Rail Class 92s

92005 (472 005), previously used by DB Cargo in Romania, was sold to Russian company LocoTech in late-2017 and was leased to Croatian operator Transagent Špedicija (TaŠ). It arrived in Croatia on 20 November 2017, and was seen outside the Hrvatske Željeznice depot at Zagreb Ranžimi Kolodvor on 13 December 2017 following modifications to meet Croatian requirements.

The modifications included new heavy-duty snow ploughs, additional grab rails and footsteps for use by shunters, new or revised external technical markings (i.e. maker ('BRUSH/ABB'), locomotive weight, brake force tonnes, wheel arrangement, axle loading, electrification warning flashes, etc) and internal cab instrumentation labels changed to Croatian. Following these modifications 92005 was ready for testing and driver training. On 12 January 2018, TaŠ conducted test runs with 92005 involving a light engine run from Rijeka through to Škrljevo, and then to the port of Bakar. From Bakar it hauled a 1030-tonne freight along the steeply graded route to Lokve with two Croatian Railways (HŽ) Cargo locomotives dead in train. 92005 finally received approval for use in Croatia in late-May 2018.

The next locomotive, 92002 (472 003-9), arrived in Croatia from Romania in March 2018, being transferred to Zagreb RK and received the same modifications as 92005 (472 005). 92012 (472 001 and 92024 (472 004) moved to Croatia in July 2018.

It is believed that 472 002 and 472 006, together with 92003/26 (after full refurbishment), were also due to follow the previous four Class 92s to Croatia. However, it now appears that the contract with LocoTech was curtailed after four locomotives.

Following sale by DB to LocoTech, 472 001/003-005 were leased to Transagent Špedicija (TaŠ), later named Transagent Rail (TaR). They retained their Romanian EVN numbers albeit with their previous Romanian names removed; the DB red livery (with DB logos) was also initially retained in Croatia by 472 003 and 005, although by 12 August 2018, 472 005 had received a special chequered dark-blue/black livery (applied using vinyls) with large 'TRANSAGENT RAIL' markings. 472 001 and 472 004 received the new TaR livery before entry into revenue-earning service (i.e. curved black and white stripes applied using vinyls at each end of the bodyside over the DB red base livery, together with 'TRANSAGENT RAIL' markings in the central bodyside red section).

The primary workload for the Class 92s is the movement of coal from the port of Bakar to Gyékényes on the Hungarian border; authorisation for their use on these trains through to the final Budapest destination in Hungary is a TaR objective.

Summary:-

Loco No./EVN	UK No.	Ex-Romania	Prepared at	Liveries/logos (with dates noted)
91 53 0 472 001-3	92012	05/07/18	DB, Turceni/HŽ Zagreb RK	DB DBlogo(b+f) ce <u>nd</u> Ooo bn(x2)+fn (16/08/18), then TaR Large TaRlogo (b) ce nd Ooo bn(x2)+fn (xx/10/18)

Observations en route Croatia: Szolnok (HU): 06/07/18.
Noted: Zagreb area (undergoing certification tests) 16/08/18 (modified).

| 91 53 0 472 003-9 | 92002 | 22/03/18 | DB, Turceni/HŽ Zagreb RK | DB DBlogo(b+f) ce CEd Ooo cn+bn+fn (23/06/18 and 21/08/18) |

Noted: Zagreb RK depot 08/05/18 (unmodified)

| 91 53 0 472 004-7 | 92024 | 05/07/18 | DB, Turceni/HŽ Zagreb RK | DB DBlogo(b+f) ce <u>nd</u> Ooo bn+fn (22/08/18 and 27/08/18), then
TaR Large TaRlogo (b) ce nd Ooo bn(x1)+fn (03/09/18)
TaR Large TaRlogo (b) ce nd Ooo bn(x2)+fn (xx/10/18) |

Observations en route Croatia: Szolnok (HU): 06/07/18.
Noted: Zagreb RK depot 22/08/18 (modified) and 27/08/18.

| 91 53 0 472 005-4 | 92005 | 20/11/17 | DB, Turceni/HŽ Zagreb RK | DB DBlogo(b+f) ce CEd Ooo cn+bn+fn (xx/12/17 and 30/05/18), then
DB Small TaRlogo(b) ce CEd Ooo cn+bn+fn (19/07/18), then
TaR(Spec) Large TaRlogo(b) ce nd Ooo fn(only) (12/08/18) |

Noted: Zagreb RK depot 23/11/17 (unmodified)+13/12/17 (modified), Dugo Selo xx/12/17, Trials (Rijeka-Lokve) 12/01/18, Rijeka 30/01/18 (under repair).

Abbreviations:

Livery details:	ce: Cabside BR double-arrow emblems, CEd: Crewe Electric depot diamond plates, nd: No depot plates, Ooo: Channel Tunnel roundels, cn: cabside numbers, bn: bodyside numbers, fn: front-end numbers.
Logo position:	b: bodyside, f: front.

92002 (472 003-9), Skrljevo, 21 August 2018. Stabled between duties. Note the additional Croatian appendages, including new grab-rails and steps, new overhead electric wire signage and extra hieroglyphics on the bodyside. However, the DB red livery and logos have been retained, at least in the short term.

92005 (472 005-4), Skrljevo, 23 August 2018. A comparison of British-built Class 92 and local Class 1141 electrics.

92005 (472 005-4), Skrljevo, 21 August 2018. This locomotive originally operated in Croatia in the DB red livery, but subsequently changed to this dark-blue/black chequered livery to celebrate the achievements of the Croatian national football team in the 2018 World Cup.

92005 (472 005-4), Bakar, 23 August 2018. A Transagent Rail Class 92 transferring a rake of empty box-wagons from Skrljevo to Bakar port for re-loading with coal for Hungary.

92024 (472 004-7), Zagreb Ranžimi Kolodvor depot, 22 August 2018. The RK freight depot at Zagreb carried out the requisite commissioning work prior to Class 92 introduction in Croatia.